OCR HISTORY A

Mid-Tudor Crises 1536–69

Nick Fellows | Series Editors: Nick Fellows and Mike Wells

www.heinemann.co.uk

✓ Free online support
✓ Useful weblinks
✓ 24 hour online ordering

0845 630 33 33

Heinemann

Part of Pearson

Heinemann is an imprint of Pearson Education Limited, a company incorporated in England and Wales, having its registered office at Edinburgh Gate, Harlow, Essex, CM20 2JE. Registered company number: 872828

www.heinemann.co.uk

Heinemann is a registered trademark of Pearson Education Limited

Text © Nick Fellows, 2010

First published 2010

12 11 10 09 08

10 9 8 7 6 5 4 3 2 1

British Library Cataloguing in Publication Data

A catalogue record for this book is available from the Britsh Library

ISBN 978 0435 312 688

Acknowledgements

Photographs and images

The author and publisher would like to thank the following for their kind permission to reproduce their photographs:

Figure 1.1 Mirza Ahmed Photography; Figure 1.2, 1.4 Roger Wade-Walker; Figure 1.3 Mike Booth; Figure 2.1 Pictorial Press; Figure 2.3 Bridgeman Art Library: Private Collection/ © Richard Philip, London; Figure 2.4 Society of Antiquaries of London; Figure 2.5 Gustavo Tomsich; Figures 2.6, 2.7, 3.2 London Art Archive; Figure 3.1 Classic Image; Figure 3.3 Alamy Images: Angelo Hornak; Figure 3.4 TopFoto; Figure 4.2 City of London/HIP; Source X Fotomas; Figures 4.3, 5.1 Mark Walker; Figure 5.2 Corbis: Bettmann; Figure 5.4 The Art Archive: Private Collection/Philip Mould; Figure 5.5 Philip Mould Ltd

Written sources

The author and publishers would like to thank the following copyright holders for permission to reproduce the following extracts:

p9 Source A *The English*, G E Elton, Wiley-Blackwell; p9, 155 Source B *Authority and Disorder in Tudor Times, 1485–1603*, P Thomas, 1999, Cambridge University Press; p9 Source C *The Emergence of a Nation State 1529–1660*, A Smith, Pearson; p9 Source D *The Tudor Years*, 2nd edition, ed J Lotherington, Hodder Education; p33, 54, 93 *The Later Reformation in England 1547–1603*, D MacCulloch, Palgrave Macmillan; p51, 152 *The Government Policy of Protector Somerset*, M L Bush, Edward Arnold; p58, *The 'Anonymous Life' of William Cecil, Lord Burghley*, A G R Smith, Edwin Mellen Press Ltd, p66, 69, 72, 87, 94 *English Reformations: Religion, Politics and Society under the Tudors*, C Haigh, Oxford University Press; p72, 81, 152 *Mid Tudor Crisis, 1545–1565*, D Loades, Palgrave Macmillan; p79 *The Local Impact of the Tudor Reformations*, R Hutton, 1987, Cambridge University Press; p87 *The Later Tudors*, P Williams, Oxford University Press, p94 *The Reign of Elizabeth: England 1558–1603*, B Mervyn, John Murray; p104 *Edward VI and Mary: A Mid-Tudor Crisis?*, N Heard, Hodder Education; p121 *Introduction to Tudor England, 1485–1603*, T Imperato & A Anderson, Hodder Education; p127 BBC A Level History, J Fines, The Historical Assocation; p148 Source X *Tudor Rebellions*, A Fletcher, Pearson; p148 Source Y, p153 *Elizabeth I*, C Haigh, Pearson

Every effort has been made to contact copyright holders of material reproduced in this book. Any omissions will be rectified in subsequent printings if notice is given to the publishers.

Contents

How to use this book

Notes for teachers

This book, *OCR History A, Mid-Tudor Crises 1536–69*, is designed to support OCR's History A F963 Option A Topic 2 Enquiries specification. After an introductory chapter, which provides the factual context of the period leading up to 1536 and an overview of the subsequent period, there are four chapters related to the four key issues of the OCR specification. These chapters are intended to cover the main elements of the indicative content set out by OCR.

Enquiries

In the OCR examination, candidates are required to compare sources as evidence, and there are opportunities to practise this skill throughout the book.

Candidates also have to use a set of sources to evaluate an interpretation. In order to help them develop the skills of interpreting sources, applying their own knowledge to assess the sources, and reaching a conclusion about the issue to which the sources relate, there are exercises which are stepped in difficulty. As a result, not all of the activities are in the format of the OCR papers, but they all aim to lead students towards the critical consideration of a set of four or five sources.

Help is given with identifying issues that candidates are likely to have to discuss. Though historians' views have been included, the AS paper is not focused on historiography or the different interpretations of historians, but on issues in which evidence may conflict. For example, historian's views of the idea of a mid-Tudor crisis are considered in the introduction and there are different interpretations of the progress of the Reformation. Contemporary sources are used to show the different views of the time. Their viewpoints are likely to be different depending on the nature, origin and the date of the source.

Advice is given about using sources as evidence and activities are focused on areas of possible discussion. Because many of the issues of the period are controversial there is plenty of conflicting evidence given here. In the examination there may be four or five sources; only one at most will be from a historian, and it is possible that all will be primary sources. Thus it is very important that students have the opportunity to evaluate a range of sources and to test the evidence they provide by using a variety of criteria, including contextual knowledge.

This book cannot be a comprehensive account of the mid-Tudor period, but teachers should remember that candidates are expected to use contextual knowledge in relation to source evaluation. Candidates are not expected to have a very detailed knowledge of every aspect of the political, religious, social and economic developments, but rather to develop the skills of source evaluation and an understanding of the key issues.

Source exercises

The activities are based on two different types of exercise:

- Comparison of two sources as evidence for a specific issue – type (a) questions in the exam, with marks out of 30. Students should assess content and provenance and be able to compare the two with a sense of judgement.

- Evaluation and interpretation of a number of sources as evidence for an issue – type (b) questions in the exam, with marks out of 70. Candidates are encouraged to group sources rather than deal with them sequentially and to apply a range of critical criteria and knowledge gained by reading the text. The sources used are cited and there is a bibliography for further reading. There is, of course, a huge literature on the mid-Tudor period, so some teacher guidance will be necessary. There is such a lot of good historical writing that it is hoped that students will be stimulated to read further.

Please note: the sources in this book, for the most part, are longer than those used in the examination.

Exam support

Each chapter also has detailed exam preparation and support in the *Exam Café* on pages 162–175.

Exam Café focuses on the type of questions assessed in the exam. It is divided into three areas: Relax, Refresh, Result!

- Relax is an area for sharing revision tips.
- Refresh your memory is an area for revising content.
- Result is the examiner's area: it includes exam questions, student answers with examiner comments, and tips on how to achieve a higher level answer.

OCR History A, Mid-Tudor Crises 1536–69 has been written specifically to provide teachers and students with a taught course that exactly reflects the key issues and skills in the specification topics. Each chapter begins with key questions on a key issue from the specification, which are then discussed in the chapter, with supporting activities.

Additionally, selected chapters include a timeline which gives an overview of the period's chronology. In conclusion, each chapter has a final review of what has been learned, together with some review questions to help student's self assessment of their knowledge.

Methods of assessment

This book supports British history Enquiries Unit F963, Option A. This is a document study paper of 1.5 hours and is worth 50% of the total AS marks. Four or five unseen sources are set. There are two questions for each study topic. Question (a) is worth 30 marks and question (b) is worth 70 marks. The *Mid-Tudor Crises 1536–69* study topic must be taken with an AS Period Studies paper on European and World History.

Thanks

The author would like to thank his family for their support during the writing of this book. It is dedicated to the memory of his mother and father who both died during its completion.

Notes for students

This book has been specifically written to support you through the OCR A GCE History course. *OCR History A, Mid-Tudor Crises 1536–69* will help you to understand the facts and concepts that underlie the topics you are studying. It can be used as a reference throughout your course.

You should refer back to this book during your revision. The Exam Café sections at the end of each unit will be particularly helpful as you prepare for your exam.

Each chapter in the book makes use of the following features:

Activities

The activities have been designed to help you understand the specification content and develop your historical skills.

> **ACTIVITY**
>
> Read Source GG and answer the following questions.
>
> 1 What reasons does Thomas give for the failure of the Pilgrimage?
>
> 2 How far do you agree with his interpretation? Why?

Biography

Short biographies of the key people from the time period you are studying.

> **BIOGRAPHY**
>
> **Charles V**
>
> King of Spain, Holy Roman Emperor and as such the most powerful ruler in Europe. Although his power in the Empire was limited and the French sometimes allied with the Pope against him, it was very difficult for the Pope to ignore his wishes.

Definitions

Definitions of new words can be found in the margin next to where the word appears in the text to help put the word in context. All definitions can also be found in the Glossary (p. 178).

> **Dry Stamp**
>
> A stamp of the royal signature. It could be printed on documents and inked over by clerks. At the end of Henry's reign it was used to sign documents without the King's knowledge, allowing Somerset to exercise a great deal of power.

Examiner's advice

Advice from the experts on how to avoid common mistakes and achieve the best possible mark in your exam.

> **Examiner's advice**
>
> It is important that you do not just skim-read sources, but read them carefully and ensure that you understand the content. As you read Source A below, ensure that you are clear about the order of succession and the authority by which the succession was to be determined.

Information

You should be thinking like an historian throughout your history course. These highlight content to provide extra detail to the historical narrative in the chapter.

> **Dissolution of the Smaller Monasteries**
>
> This Act closed down all monasteries with an income of less than £200 per year, resulting in the closure of about 285 monasteries out of 850.

Sources

We have included lots of sources throughout the book to allow you to practise your historical skills.
Note: the sources tend to be longer than they would be in the exam.

Stretch and challenge

These activities pull together work done giving you practice in the skills needed for your final exam.

Exam support

In our unique *Exam Café* on pages 162–175 you'll find lots of ideas to help prepare for your exams.

You can **Relax** because there's handy revision advice from fellow students; **Refresh your Memory** with summaries and checklists of the key ideas you need to revise, and **Get that Result!** through practising exam-style questions, accompanied by hints and tips on getting the very best grades.

Source

(F) *To win the throne, Mary relied on a small group of Catholic gentry supporters, but the secret of her success was a much wider appeal to legitimacy and a careful avoidance of religious issues during the course of the crisis itself.*

D. MacCulloch (1990) *The Later Reformation in England 1547–1603*. Macmillan.

Stretch and challenge

Compare the views put forward in Sources DD and EE on the impact of the Marian persecutions. (Note that you will not be asked to compare the views of two modern historians in the exam.)

ExamCafé
Relax, refresh, result!

The period from 1536 to 1569 has fascinated both historians and the general public. This is partly because of the personalities of two of the monarchs who ruled during this period, Henry VIII and Elizabeth I, but also because of the vast number of changes that England underwent, particularly in religion. There are also many sites associated with these rulers, ranging from the royal palace at Hampton Court to the monasteries that were closed down by Henry. These help students to gain a much deeper understanding of the period. All the monarchs of the period – Henry VIII, Edward VI, Mary Tudor and Elizabeth – are figures who have attracted both love and hatred.

Figure 1.1   Henry VIII's palace at Hampton Court.

This book will offer you the chance to look closely at the evidence of the time and the views of historians, to make your own judgements on the main issues and to practise and develop the historical skills necessary, with regard to source interpretation and evaluation, to achieve the maximum possible in your examination.

In this chapter there is background information to the period which will help you to understand what had been happening in the period before 1536 so that you can see how events developed and understand the background to the changes that were taking place. There is also an overview of the whole period.

The mid-Tudor crises

Why is the period 1536 to 1569 seen as a series of crises? In order to start to answer this question you need to think about what is meant by the term 'crisis'. In this context it is usually seen to be a point at which the state, the Church, society and economy came close to collapse. There is certainly evidence to suggest that the period was one of difficulties in many areas, and it is around these that this book is based.

- the monarchy and its ministers
- religious change
- economic and social change
- social unrest.

The book will encourage you to ask how close to collapse England came as a result of events and developments in the four areas listed above. You will be encouraged to develop your own conclusions, making not just overall judgements, but judgements about the challenges presented by individual events. You should be willing to modify and change your answers as you develop your understanding of the period, and be aware that historians still disagree about the scale of the difficulties and problems.

Sources

Read the following extracts from modern historians.

A *Two real crises did occur in the sixteenth century. The first in the 1540s and 1550s sprang from a massive inflation of prices. The second was the rebellions of 1549, which arose from the complex of economic difficulties and social distress.*

G.R. Elton (1992) *The English*. Blackwell.

In which aspects of society do Elton and Thomas suggest that there were crises? Do they agree on the areas? **What does this suggest to you about the term 'the mid-Tudor crises'?**

B *Was there a crisis in religion between 1547 and 1563? Given the confusion, rebellion, plotting and faction that religious change created, it is hard to deny that there was indeed a crisis. It is quite clear that religious change struck at the heart of traditional concepts of authority, at high and low, central and local level.*

P. Thomas (1999) *Authority and Disorder in Tudor Times 1485–1603*. CUP.

Sources

Now read two more extracts from historians:

C *It is doubtful if the Tudor State was ever in quite as serious difficulties as the word 'crisis' implies. Between 1540 and 1558 the throne was occupied successively by a sick and rapidly ageing bully, a boy who was too young to rule and a woman of limited political abilities. In these circumstances what is significant and remarkable is not the weakness of government, but its relative strength.*

A. Smith (1997) *The Emergence of a Nation State 1529–1660*. Longman.

D *The crisis theory overlooks the fact that the government never lost control, even in 1549. This may have been partly because the two rebellions in 1549 had limited aims and did not intend to topple the government. The Council functioned effectively from 1540 despite undoubted factional turmoil from time to time. The governing elites survived the most dangerous moment in 1553 when they decided to back Mary's legitimate descent.*

E. Towne (1994) in *The Tudor Years*, ed. J. Lotherington. Hodder.

Stretch and challenge

Read Sources A–D. Although in the exam you would not be required to consider the views of four historians, these extracts show that the debate is still alive today.

1   What do these historians think about the idea of 'mid-Tudor crises'?

2   Do they agree on why the period should not be seen as a period of crisis?

3   Having read these extracts, what do you think? Why?

Although this is only your initial view and you should be prepared to change it as you develop a deeper understanding of the period, it is important that you start to form a judgement about the key question.

The early Tudor years, 1485–1529

The first of the Tudors had gained the throne by defeating and killing Richard III at the Battle of Bosworth in 1485. Henry VII's claim was very weak and he spent much of his reign securing the throne and restoring order after the civil war that had gripped England over the previous 30 years. Henry was also able to restore the royal finances so that when he died in 1509 the Crown was solvent.

Henry VII was succeeded by his son, Henry VIII. One of the new king's first acts was to marry his dead brother's wife, Catherine of Aragon. This marriage would have considerable consequences for the monarchy and the people of England. Henry VIII was not like his father. His youth and ambition were a clear change from the insecurity of Henry VII. He was a true prince of the Renaissance, enjoying sport, hunting, music and warfare. It did not take long for him to exhaust the royal treasury as he tried, though with little success, to revive the old English claim to the French throne. At home, as he was less interested in the day-to-day running of the country, much of the business of government was left to his principal advisor, Cardinal Thomas Wolsey. Wolsey had risen from virtual obscurity, the son of an Ipswich butcher, to be Henry's chief advisor following his successful organisation of the first war in France. His lowly origins created jealousy among many of the nobles, who were waiting for an opportunity to get their own back at this upstart.

Trouble for Wolsey started in 1525 when he tried to raise large sums of money for a further campaign in France. Unrest broke out in many areas of England and Wolsey was forced to abandon his plans and make a public apology. However, it was Henry's desire for an annulment of his marriage to Catherine that was to bring about Wolsey's downfall. The marriage had produced only one surviving child, Mary, and the King was concerned about the question of the succession. Whether Henry genuinely believed that the lack of a male heir was God's punishment for marrying his brother's widow, or whether it was simply the excuse he needed to be able to ask the Pope for an annulment is a matter of debate. At the same time, Henry had fallen in love with Anne Boleyn. Unlike her sister, Anne refused to become the King's mistress, insisting that she would sleep with him only when she was queen. All these events put pressure on Wolsey as papal legate to obtain an annulment so that Henry could marry Anne. Unfortunately for Wolsey, the task was virtually impossible, as the Pope was a virtual prisoner of **Charles V**. Charles was Catherine's nephew and would never allow the annulment to be granted as it would be a humiliation for his family. Despite these difficulties, the Boleyns and many others who disliked Wolsey's monopoly of power convinced Henry that Wolsey was to blame for the failure. Henry was only too willing to listen and his chief minister was soon stripped of his titles, but escaped further punishment by dying as he travelled back to London.

BIOGRAPHY

Charles V

King of Spain, Holy Roman Emperor and as such the most powerful ruler in Europe. Although his power in the Empire was limited and the French sometimes allied with the Pope against him, it was very difficult for the Pope to ignore his wishes.

The impact of the break with Rome, 1529–36

Wolsey's removal did not bring a solution to Henry's problem any closer. He used Parliament to put pressure on the Pope by threatening to stop payments to the papacy, but to no avail. The situation changed dramatically at the start of 1533: Anne was pregnant and an annulment became vital. Henry could not afford for the child to be illegitimate, particularly if it was male, therefore a solution to Henry's matrimonial difficulties had to be found. In solving the problem, two men emerged as new favourites to replace Wolsey: Thomas Cromwell and Thomas Cranmer. Cromwell piloted legislation through Parliament that resulted in England breaking away from the Roman Catholic Church; Cranmer pronounced Henry's marriage to Catherine annulled and performed his marriage to Anne. Table 1.1 summarises the changes that took place in the years 1533–36 and will give you a clear understanding of the situation when your period of study starts.

Date	Event	Impact
1533	Act in Restraint of Appeals	This prevented people in England from appealing to the Pope on religious matters such as divorce. It also meant that England was a completely independent state, free from papal interference
1533	Act in Restraint of Annates	This stopped some payments to Rome, but more importantly, it gave the king the right to appoint bishops
1533	Dispensations Act	This stopped all payments to Rome
1533	Act for the Submission of the Clergy	This gave the king control over the Church's parliament and prevented any appeals to the Pope, even in religious matters
1534	The Act of Supremacy	This Act recognised Henry as head of the Church in England and gave him influence over its doctrine and beliefs
1534	Act of Succession	This ended any claim by Catherine to be Henry's wife and declared Mary illegitimate. Henry's marriage to Anne was declared lawful and any criticism was treason; children of the Boleyn marriage were the lawful heirs
1534	Act for First Fruits and Tenths	Those who were appointed to posts in the Church had to give some of their income to the king
1534	The Treason Act	This made it treason to criticise Henry for any changes he had made in the Church

Table 1.1 The changes that took place in the years 1533–36.

Despite the break with the Roman Catholic Church, the doctrine and beliefs of the English Church remained unchanged in these years. What had changed, however, was the jurisdictional power of the king over the Church.

One of the more challenging parts of the AS course is understanding the changing nature of religious beliefs that occurred as a result of the Reformation. When Henry VIII came to the throne, everyone in England was Catholic and owed obedience to the Pope in Rome.

What did the Catholic Church teach?

- The Pope was the head of the Church.
- The mass was the most important service. It was said by the priest in Latin, and people were expected to attend church every Sunday and on Holy Days to hear it. The most important part of the service was the Eucharist, when the priest said prayers over the bread and wine.
- At mass, the bread and wine, although outwardly appearing the same, actually became the body and blood of Christ. This was known as transubstantiation.
- Only the priest received both the bread and wine; the congregation received only bread.
- After death, a person's soul might go to heaven or hell for eternity. They could only go to heaven if they were free from sin, but most people had committed some sins so would go to purgatory.
- People needed to perform 'good works' in order to avoid going to hell.
- There was a 'halfway house' between hell and heaven, known as purgatory. In order to be purged of the sins they had committed on earth, souls of the dead would spend time in purgatory, depending upon how great their sins were.
- Souls could spend less time in purgatory if people prayed for them. People had special chapels, known as chantries, built so that masses could be said for them after their death.
- There were seven sacraments which gave the receiver special grace: Eucharist, Baptism, Confirmation, Marriage, Penance, Holy Orders (for someone who was becoming a priest) and Extreme Unction (for people who were dying).
- People should undertake pilgrimages (journeys to places of religious significance); this would help them get to heaven.
- Monasteries were valuable, providing places of prayer, centres of charity, education and care.
- Holy Days were days off work to celebrate the festivals of saints.
- Relics were religious objects such as bones of saints or pieces of the cross. Religious centres often had collections of such objects and people made pilgrimages to pray at them.
- Churches contained many images of saints, and people addressed prayers to them.
- Priests could not marry, and should remain celibate.

Figure 1.2   A Catholic church.

KEY
1   Rood screen
2   Sanctuary lamps
3   Server
4   Surplice
5   Hanging tabernacle
6   Missal
7   Altar
8   Priest
9   Alb
10 Chasuble
11 Reredos
12 Cross with statues of St John
    (right) and Virgin Mary (left)
13 Chalice
14 Stained glass window
15 Wall painting

The dominance of Catholic teachings had been challenged in Germany in 1517 by Martin Luther. His ideas resulted in the establishment of Protestantism in a number of countries across Europe from the 1520s onwards. Henry VIII had attacked Luther's teachings and beliefs in a book and as a result he had received the title 'Defender of the Faith' from the Pope. It was therefore quite ironic that he had broken all his links with the papacy, but it may also explain why Henry remained attached to most of the Catholic beliefs outlined on page 12.

What did Protestants believe?

It is important that you understand these key beliefs, as only then will you be able to judge whether England was becoming more Protestant.

- People needed to have genuine faith to go to heaven; this was known as 'justification by faith alone' or *sola fide*.
- They did not accept the Pope as head of the Church.
- Services should be in English, not in Latin.
- The Bible was the centre of people's beliefs, and not the Catholic Church's interpretation of it.
- The Bible should be in English so that everyone, not just the priest, could read it.
- Good works alone did not get a person to heaven; they had to have faith.
- They did not believe in the doctrine of purgatory.
- At the Eucharist the bread and wine did not change and the service was a remembrance of Christ's sacrifice.
- The congregation received both bread and wine.

- People could talk directly to God and did not need a priest as an intermediary, hence the belief in the 'priesthood of all believers'.
- There was a greater emphasis on the preaching and teaching role of priests. This meant that an educated priesthood was needed.
- There was no value in pilgrimages.
- The Catholic Church's worship of saints was seen as an unnecessary digression from communication with God, and there was too much emphasis on the Virgin Mary. The number of Holy Days was therefore reduced.
- The monastic life was without value.
- There was no value in relics or images.
- Priests should be allowed to marry.

Figure 1.3   A chantry chapel.

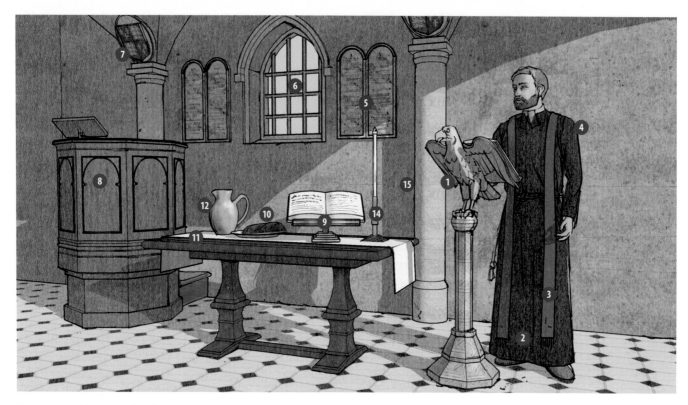

Figure 1.4   A Protestant church.

Although the changes in the years 1529–35 had done nothing to change Church doctrine, it did not mean that everyone accepted them. Despite the Treason Act, a number of people opposed the divorce and the Royal Supremacy, most notably Thomas More, John Fisher and Carthusian monks from the Charterhouse. Henry could not allow opposition from such prominent individuals, and as a result they were put to death. It was the Dissolution of the Smaller Monasteries in 1536 (see Chapter 3, page 62) that brought home to ordinary people the significance of the changes and led to the first major rebellion of the period, the Pilgrimage of Grace (see Chapter 5, pages 126–130). This rebellion was also an attack on Henry's new chief minister, Thomas Cromwell (see Chapter 2, pages 45–48), who was believed to be behind many of the changes.

It is very important that you understand the significance of the changes that took place in this period, as they provide the background for many of the developments that took place in the years 1536–69.

- They laid the foundations for the religious conflicts and provided the motivation for some of the rebellions.
- They added a new, religious dimension to the factional struggles between those in and out of favour.
- They had an impact on foreign policy, which would have a knock-on effect on the economy as monarchs looked to raise the large sums of money needed to fight wars.

At the same time, other changes added to the problems that governments would face.

- The population was starting to grow; this would put pressure on food supplies and increase the cost of living.

KEY

1   'Eagle' lectern for Bible
2   Surplice
3   Scarf of silk
4   Priest
5   Wall tablets containing the Ten Commandments
6   Plain glass in window
7   Royal coat-of-arms
8   Pulpit for preaching
9   Book of Common Prayer at north end of table. The priest stands there at communion service
10 Ordinary bread
11 White linen cloth
12 Flagon of wine

- The development of printing and rising rates of literacy meant that new ideas could spread more quickly.
- English trade with the continent brought new ideas from Europe.

Changes 1536–40

Many thought that with the death of Catherine of Aragon in 1536, Henry would be reconciled with Rome, but this did not happen. Instead, Henry continued his matrimonial exploits: Anne Boleyn, who had failed to provide a male heir, was arrested and executed for alleged adultery in 1536 and within weeks Henry married Jane Seymour. The marriage was short as Jane died in 1538, but she did provide Henry with his son, Edward. Meanwhile, religious changes continued as Henry's chief minister, Thomas Cromwell, brought in brought in measures that set out a more Protestant view of the Church, including the dissolution of the monasteries. However, there were limits to how far Henry was willing to allow these developments. This was made clear in 1538 when John Lambert was convicted for denying transubstantiation (see page 12) and a proclamation was issued against heresy. This was followed in 1539 by the Act of Six Articles, which reversed nearly all of the changes in religious doctrine.

The Catholics at court saw their opportunity and increased their attacks on Cromwell. He might have survived but for the failure of Henry's fourth marriage. On Cromwell's advice, to secure a Protestant alliance against the threat of a Catholic crusade, Henry had married Anne of Cleves, daughter of the German Duke of Cleves. The marriage was a disaster and Cromwell was blamed by the Catholics, who twisted Henry's ear to their view and also introduced the young Catherine Howard to his attentions. The Catholics also suggested that Cromwell was protecting a group of Protestants in Calais. He was arrested and executed in June 1540.

Years of faction and royal weakness, 1540–47

With Cromwell's death, Henry did not appoint a new chief minister. Instead he chose to rule by himself. As he became older, conflict between the conservative, Catholic faction and the reformist, Protestant faction dominated his reign and weakened royal authority. Henry's marriage to Catherine Howard was short-lived as the reform faction was soon able to produce evidence of her adultery and she was executed in 1542, along with some of the conservative faction. Henry married Catherine Parr, his sixth and final wife, in 1544. Religious policy in the period appeared uncertain as there were apparent moves back towards Catholicism with the King's Book and the Act for the Advancement of True Religion (see Chapter 3, pages 68–69), but there were also apparent moves towards Protestantism with the English Litany. These developments were complicated by the factional struggle which saw the conservatives accuse first Cranmer of heresy and then members of the queen's household. Both survived because of Henry's intervention. However, when the reformers turned on the conservatives they achieved success, removing Stephen Gardiner and having the Duke of Norfolk and his son arrested.

By the time of Henry's death in 1547 the reform faction was dominant. The reformers had control of the **Dry Stamp** and used their position to alter Henry's will. As a result, the reformers were able to dominate the Council and despite Henry's plan to stop any single group achieving total control, this was undone within three days of his death: Edward's uncle, Seymour, was made Lord Protector and took the title Duke of Somerset. The ageing tyrant appeared to have given way to minority rule.

Dry Stamp

A stamp of the royal signature. It could be printed on documents and inked over by clerks. At the end of Henry's reign it was used to sign documents without the King's knowledge, allowing Somerset to exercise a great deal of power.

The rule of a boy king, 1547–53

Already social and economic problems were developing as a result of the population rise and the ambitious foreign policy pursued by Henry in the 1540s. This had resulted in the debasement of the coinage and the sale of Crown lands to finance the war, creating financial instability. Conditions for the peasantry were made worse in some areas of the country as landowners followed a policy of enclosure, which often resulted in the peasantry losing access to common land (see Chapter 4).

These problems were made worse by weak royal authority, the result of having a minor on the throne and the inevitable factional conflict that followed. Henry had also left a situation of religious instability. Attempts to resolve some of these problems created further unrest. Religious reforms that were moderately Protestant (see Chapter 3, page 72) caused rebellion in the West Country (see Chapter 5, page 131). Policies designed to lessen the economic difficulties encouraged the peasantry to rise (see Chapter 5, pages 133–134), with the result that the summer of 1549 saw rebellion in much of southern and eastern England.

It was this that gave Somerset's opponents the opportunity to strike, and in October 1549 he was removed from power. The struggle that followed finally saw the emergence of John Dudley, Duke of Northumberland, as the triumphant force. He restored order to the country and strengthened the value of the currency after debasement, but also introduced religious reforms that took England further down the Protestant road, culminating in the Second Prayer Book of 1552 and the Forty-Two Articles.

However, it was the health of the young king that had the most dramatic impact on events. At the start of 1553, Edward's health went into decline and it soon became apparent that he was not going to recover. The heir to the throne was his half-sister Mary, a known Catholic. Attempts were made to alter the succession to prevent her acceding to the throne, and to preserve the position of Northumberland and his supporters (see Chapter 2, page 32).

With Edward's death in July 1553, Lady Jane Grey, who had married Northumberland's son, was proclaimed queen. This did not last. Within nine days Mary had taken the throne and arrested many of those who had tried to exclude her: England had its first female ruler for over 400 years.

The rule of a woman and Catholic restoration, 1553–58

Mary believed that her success in gaining the throne was because of both her own and the country's religious beliefs and not because she was the legitimate ruler. As a result, she thought that she could move quickly to restore England to the Catholic Church. She was unaware of the economic and social problems that the country faced and appeared solely concerned with the restoration of Catholicism.

The restoration of Catholicism went fairly smoothly; England was reconciled to Rome and the arrival of Cardinal Pole appeared to secure the link with the papacy. Mary was unable to restore monasteries and monastic land (see Chapter 3, pages 83–85) and achieve a full restoration of the Church to the pre-1529 situation. Her desire to eliminate heresy and the resultant burnings of Protestants, including Cranmer and other bishops, did much to dampen enthusiasm and damage her reputation. Closely linked to her religious zeal was her desire to marry and produce an heir so that the throne would not pass to her Protestant half-sister, Elizabeth. However, her marriage in 1554 to Philip of Spain was unpopular with many, and fear of Spanish domination resulted in Wyatt's Rebellion (see Chapter 5, pages 138–139).

The marriage failed to produce any children and England was dragged into a war against France, which appeared to be purely for Spanish interests and resulted in the loss of Calais, the last piece of English territory on the continent. At the same time, Mary's last years were characterised by a disastrous economic situation as harvests repeatedly failed and sickness and influenza killed off a large part of the population. Although Mary did not want Elizabeth, the Protestant daughter of Anne Boleyn, to succeed to the throne and change the religion of the country, she ultimately accepted that, as in her situation, legitimacy, rather than religious belief, would have to triumph. Consequently, when Mary died in 1558 it was Elizabeth who succeeded to the throne. Mary's death was greeted with a sense of relief, although questions about Elizabeth's legitimacy meant that her long-term survival was not secure.

Elizabeth's early years, 1558–69

Elizabeth was a complete contrast to Mary. She was much more self-confident and took a far less emotional approach to government. If Mary was driven by her emotional attachment to her faith, Elizabeth took a much more pragmatic approach. She was also clearly her father's daughter, believing in strong government, which was vital if she was to survive the problems she faced.

> **Source**
>
> (E) **The following passage was written by Armigail Waad, a former Clerk to the Privy Council under Edward VI. This is an extract from his work 'The Distresses of the Commonwealth, with the means to remedy them.'**
>
> *The Queen poor, the realm exhausted, the nobility poor and decayed. Lack of good captains and soldiers. The people out of order. Justice is not executed. All things are dear. Divisions among ourselves. Wars with France and Scotland. The French king bestriding the realm, having one foot in Calais and the other in Scotland. Steadfast enmity but no steadfast friendship abroad.*

What problems did Elizabeth face on her accession?

In order to secure the succession it was expected that Elizabeth would marry, and these issues dominated the early years of her reign as both the Privy Council and Parliament pushed her to make a decision. This was made even more urgent when she suffered a near-fatal attack of smallpox in 1562. However, Elizabeth continued to resist and the issue would drag on throughout her reign as she refused to name a successor (see Chapter 2, pages 34–36).

The religious situation was equally complex, since England was still legally Catholic, as were many of its people, but as a Protestant, Elizabeth was seen as illegitimate by many Catholics. Her first years saw her negotiate a moderately Protestant religious settlement through Parliament, which aimed at avoiding the alienation of moderate Catholics (see Chapter 3, pages 90–96). In this she was largely successful and it was not until 1569, when the question of the succession and religion combined in the form of Mary Stuart's presence in England, that she faced rebellion in the form of the Revolt of the Northern Earls (see Chapter 5, pages 139–141). The defeat of this unrest was the last serious challenge to the throne that she would face, and marks the end of the mid-Tudor crises.

Source

F **Read the following description of the royal progress, written by the Spanish ambassador in 1568.**

She was received everywhere with great acclamations and signs of joy, as is customary in this country; whereat she was extremely pleased and told me so, giving me to understand how beloved she was by her subjects and how highly she esteemed this, together with the fact that they were peaceful and contented, whilst her neighbours on all sides are in such trouble. She attributed it all to God's miraculous goodness. She ordered her carriage to be taken where the crowd seemed thickest, and stood up and thanked the people.

ACTIVITY

Re-read Source F.

How successful do the Spanish ambassador's comments suggest that Elizabeth was in overcoming the problems she faced?

Conclusion

As you have read this introduction you should have gained an overview of the events you are about to study. You should be considering whether there is sufficient evidence to suggest that this was a period of crisis. In order to start to reach a judgement, you should consider the following questions:

- Is there enough evidence to suggest that there was a crisis throughout the period?
- Were the crises confined to just one aspect of the period? If so, was there a political crisis? A religious crisis? A social and economic crisis?
- Were the crises confined to the rule of one monarch? If so, which one? Or were they confined to a particular year?

If you go back to the historians' comments on page 9, you will see that they have different views. Some have focused on one aspect of the period, such as religion or social and economic change. Some look back and compare the period with what happened before, or look forward and compare the period with what Elizabeth would achieve. Others have been more positive about the whole period and do not believe that the government ever faced a serious crisis, while others focus on particular aspects, such as the treatment of Protestants under Mary or the problems of the poor throughout the period. As a result there are many different perspectives for you to consider, and this is what makes the period so fascinating to study.

You should now reconsider your views in light of their judgements.

The timeline on pages 20–23 outlines the main events that you will encounter as you study the period. It will be a valuable point of reference and should help you to see the whole picture and not just the area that you are studying at any one moment.

Timeline: major developments in England 1536–69

Year	Political developments	Religious developments	Social and economic developments	Unrest
1536	Death of Catherine of Aragon Execution of Anne Boleyn Henry marries Jane Seymour	Dissolution of the smaller monasteries	Money to be raised through voluntary contributions to help the poor	Lincolnshire Rising Pilgrimage of Grace
1537				Bigod/Cumberland Rising
1538	Birth of Edward Death of Jane Seymour	Royal Injunctions		
1539		Dissolution of the larger monasteries Act of Six Articles		
1540	Henry marries Anne of Cleves Execution of Cromwell Henry marries Catherine Howard	English Bibles to be placed in all churches		
1542	Execution of Catherine Howard			
1543	Henry marries Catherine Parr Conservative plot against Cranmer	The King's Book Act for the Advancement of True Religion		
1544	Succession Act	Services to be in English	Debasement of coinage	
1545		Chantries Act passed, but not implemented		

Year	Political developments	Religious developments	Social and economic developments	Unrest
1546	Conservative plot against Catherine Parr Denny becomes Chief Gentleman of the King's Privy Chamber Henry's last will excludes Gardiner from Privy Council			
1547	Execution of Surrey Death of Henry Regency Council established with Somerset Lord Protector		Passing of Poor Law–Slavery Act Funds to be collected through churches to help poor	
1548			Enclosure Commission established	
1549	Coup removes Somerset	Act of Uniformity and First Prayer Book	Harvest failure Taxes on sheep and cloth increased	Western Rebellion Kett's Rebellion Unrest in other counties
1550	Northumberland becomes Lord President of the Council			
1551			Efforts start to strengthen currency after debasement Failed harvest Collapse in cloth exports Act setting out cloth standards	

Year	Political developments	Religious developments	Social and economic developments	Unrest
1552	Somerset executed	Second Act of Uniformity and new Prayer Book	Census to reduce unauthorised begging. People encouraged to contribute to poor relief	
1553	Devise to exclude Mary Edward dies Defeat of Jane Grey; Mary becomes queen Execution of Northumberland			Lady Jane Grey affair
1554	Mary marries Philip of Spain	Pole arrives as papal legate	Act to encourage revival of cloth-making	Wyatt's Rebellion
1555		Papal supremacy restored Pole appointed archbishop of Canterbury First execution of heretics	Bad harvest	
1556		Execution of Cranmer	Bad harvest Influenza epidemic starts	
1557		Pope deprives Pole of legateship	Act restricting cloth manufacture	
1558	Loss of Calais Death of Mary Accession of Elizabeth Cecil appointed Secretary of State			

Year	Political developments	Religious developments	Social and economic developments	Unrest
1559		Acts of Supremacy and Uniformity		
1560	Emergence of Dudley as favourite		Recoinage begins	
1562	Elizabeth ill with smallpox			
1563	Clash with Parliament over succession		Act limiting conversion of land to pasture Failure to contribute to poor relief could lead to jail Statute of Artificers	
1566	Dispute with Parliament over succession and marriage			
1568	Leicester and Norfolk plot to reduce Cecil's influence Mary Stuart forced to flee to England			
1569				Rebellion of the Northern Earls

2

How stable and well served was the monarchy in this period?

In this chapter, the main issues relate to the strength of the monarchy and how well its ministers served it. There are a number of passages for comment, interpretation and comparison: the main skill concerns interpreting and comparing sources.

- What challenges were there to the monarchy and how serious were they?
- Did faction weaken the monarchy in the period?
- How well served by its ministers was the monarchy in the period?
- Was the stability of the Tudor monarchy threatened in the period?
- What was the greatest threat to the stability of the monarchy?
- By the end of the chapter you should be aware of the problems that faced the monarchy in the period, including the issues of the succession and the problems created by the age and gender of the monarch. You will also be aware of the different explanations of the importance of faction in the period and the effectiveness of the various ministers employed by the Crown. You should be able to interpret and extract information from a range of sources and evaluate their reliability as evidence. You should also be able to deal with what they say about an issue and their value as historical evidence.

Examiner's advice

You must not forget that this is a source-based paper and therefore these issues will be examined through a series of sources from both contemporaries and historians. A study of the mark-scheme shows clearly that most of the marks are for demonstrating source skills and the focus will therefore be on developing the skills that are essential for this paper, rather than building up a detailed factual knowledge of events. These skills will be developed as you progress through the book. This chapter will focus on encouraging you to read sources carefully and think about the ways in which you can assess their provenance. This will involve thinking about issues such as who wrote the source, why it was written, its date, the language used and its typicality.

What challenges were there to the monarchy?
Did they create instability?

Three areas had the potential to threaten the stability of the monarchy in the period 1536–69. They were the issues raised by the succession of a minor and then two female rulers, the problem of faction and the abilities of the monarch's servants.

Figure 2.1 Henry VIII.

The main causes of the challenges to the monarchy were:

- Henry's complicated matrimonial exploits
- the age of the ruler
- the gender of the ruler
- the issues of marriage and the succession.

ACTIVITY

What impression does Figure 2.1 give of Henry VIII? How does the artist achieve this?

How did Henry try to solve the succession problem?

The background

As you read this section you should think about whether the succession question ever threatened the political stability of the country.

Henry VIII's marriage to Catherine of Aragon had produced only one surviving child: Mary. Many members of the ruling elites believed that the monarch must be male. Although the succession in England was not governed by **Salic Law**, there was no tradition of female rulers, and the last time a female had been named as heir, in the twelfth century, the country had collapsed into civil war. Henry probably did not believe that a female could or would be able to rule England and that a male heir was therefore essential. This was certainly a major factor in his decision to divorce Catherine and marry Anne Boleyn in 1533. The marriage to Anne resulted in a second daughter, Elizabeth, who was recognised as heir by an Act of Parliament in 1534. The same Act also declared Mary illegitimate. Following the execution of Anne in 1536 and Henry's marriage to Jane Seymour, a second Act of Succession was passed, declaring Elizabeth illegitimate.

However, the birth of a son did not secure the succession. Jane died due to complications after childbirth, and Henry subsequently married Anne of Cleves in January 1540, Catherine Howard in August 1540 and Catherine Parr in 1543. Despite these marriages no more children were born, but a Third Act of Succession was passed in 1543–44.

Salic Law

A law that had its origins in France and excluded females from succeeding to the throne

> **Examiner's advice**
>
> It is important that you do not just skim-read sources, but read them carefully and ensure that you understand the content. As you read Source A below, ensure that you are clear about the order of succession and the authority by which the succession was to be determined.

Source

 From the Third Act of Succession (1543):

In case it should happen that Henry VIII and his only son Prince Edward should die without heirs, then the crown shall pass to the Lady Mary and to her heirs, with such conditions as Henry VIII shall state by letters under the Great Seal or in his last Will; and should the Lady Mary die without heirs, then the crown shall pass to the Lady Elizabeth and to her heirs, with such conditions as Henry VIII shall state by letters under the Great Seal or in his last will.

> **ACTIVITY**
>
> 1 Why do you think Henry involved Parliament in the determining of the succession?
>
> 2 How had the order of the succession changed from the Second Act of Succession? Why?

Source

B **Henry's declining health in 1546 meant that Edward would come to the throne as a minor. Therefore, to avoid any disputes and ensure a peaceful succession, he confirmed the Third Succession Act by his will in December 1546.**

We will … that, immediately after our departure out of this present life, our said son Edward shall have and enjoy the said imperial crown and realm of England and Ireland, our title to France …

And for lack of such issue and heirs, … the said imperial crown and all other the premises shall wholly remain and come to our said daughter Mary and the heirs of her body lawfully begotten; upon condition that our said daughter Mary, after our decease [death], shall not marry nor take any person to her husband without the assent and consent of the privy councillors … We will that, after our decease, and for default of issue of … our daughter Mary [i.e. if Mary does not produce children], the said imperial crown … shall wholly remain and come to our said daughter Elizabeth and to the heirs of her body lawfully begotten…

The will also added that if all of Henry's children died without heirs the throne would pass to his niece, Frances Grey. She was the elder daughter of Henry's sister's marriage to the Duke of Suffolk. It also meant that children from Henry's elder sister Margaret's marriage to James IV of Scotland were excluded; this would mean that according to the will there was no place in the succession for **Mary Stuart (Queen of Scots)**. The will, it could be argued, was also designed to ensure that the Catholic Mary was excluded and replaced by the Protestant Grey family.

BIOGRAPHY

Mary Stuart (Queen of Scots)

The daughter of James V of Scotland and Margaret (Henry VIII's sister). Many Catholics believed she was the rightful heir as they did not recognise the validity of Henry's marriage to Anne Boleyn and therefore believed that Elizabeth was illegitimate. Mary had married the son of the King of France. She was already Queen of Scotland, but by 1559 her husband was King Francis II of France. She was therefore seen as a serious threat to English security.

ACTIVITY

1. Why did Henry's will state that if Mary should marry after Henry's death she must have the approval of the Privy Council?

2. Why do you think Henry thought it was necessary to issue instructions for the succession in his will when the Third Succession Act already existed?

3. What sources of authority have been used by Henry to settle the succession? Why?

Although both Mary and Elizabeth had been restored to the succession, the acts which had made them illegitimate were never repealed!

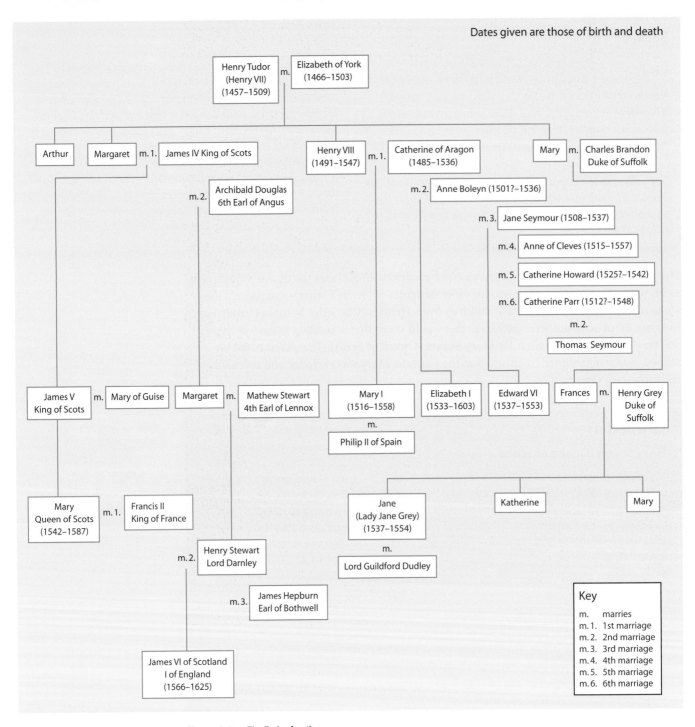

Figure 2.2 The Tudor family tree.

Although all three of Henry's children did come to the throne as the Third Act and will ordered, the succession was far from smooth.

Henry's concern for political stability had been made clear in his establishment of the Regency Council of sixteen equal members. This was to be made up of a balance between religious reformists and religious conservatives, matters were to be decided by a majority vote. However, the factional struggles of 1546 ensured that it would be Somerset and his reformist allies who triumphed (see page 30).

Figure 2.3 Edward VI.

Edward was only nine years old when he came to the throne. He was governed first by Edward Seymour, Duke of Somerset (see pages 51–52) as Lord Protector and then John Dudley, Duke of Northumberland (see pages 53–54).

How serious a threat to the power of the monarchy was Edward's age?

It must be remembered that England's record of child kings was not very encouraging:

- Richard II had succeeded to the throne in 1377 at the age of ten, but was later deposed and replaced by Henry IV.
- Henry VI had survived as king as a minor; a council of competing nobles ruled on his behalf from the time he succeeded to the throne, aged eight months, in 1422. However, civil war followed soon after he achieved majority in 1437.

■ Edward V succeeded his father, Edward IV, as king in 1483, aged 12. He was imprisoned in the Tower of London two months later, and was probably murdered, possibly by his uncle, who became Richard III.

Henry's death in 1547 brought Edward VI, a boy of nine, to the throne. Although, until his final illness in 1553, it was expected that Edward would take full control of the kingdom when he came of age, a minority nevertheless created problems that would have to be overcome.

Henry had tried to overcome these difficulties by establishing a **Regency Council** to rule the country, with all sixteen members having an equal voice. However, these provisions were quickly overthrown and Edward Seymour, uncle of the new king, soon emerged as the Duke of Somerset and Lord Protector. Despite this, there were some who questioned the legality of Somerset's authority, and this only added to the instability.

It could be argued that a council of sixteen would never have worked: it would have led to factional squabbles and unrest, and therefore a dominant voice was needed to prevent this. Yet Somerset was ambitious; he had been able to appoint supporters such as **Anthony Denny** and **William Paget** to key positions in the late king's household so that Henry's will could be altered. Then, through bribery and rewards, Somerset was able to emerge as the dominant character.

> ### Regency Council
> A group of councillors who rule on behalf of a monarch while the monarch is a child or a minor. The Regency Council of 1547–49 was headed by Somerset.

> ### What were the problems created by Edward's age?
> - inability to lead troops in war
> - emergence of faction
> - unrest and a possible return to the Wars of the Roses
> - the image of the monarchy.

> **BIOGRAPHY**
>
> **Anthony Denny**
>
> A confidant of Henry VIII, Denny was in charge of the King's Privy Chamber. This was an important role, particularly in Henry's last years, as he spent much of his time in his private rooms. People could only gain access to the King with Denny's permission, so he was able to exclude those whom he did not want to influence the King.

> **BIOGRAPHY**
>
> **William Paget**
>
> Born in 1505, Paget entered Parliament in 1529. Henry and Cranmer used him in their attempts to win support from European universities for Henry's divorce. In 1543 he became a Privy Councillor, and then Henry's Private Secretary. Along with Somerset he was Henry's main advisor in the King's final years. He supported Somerset's protectorship against Northumberland, and served both Northumberland and Mary – though he did oppose Mary's religious reforms.

There is little doubt that Somerset used his position to further his own power and wealth. He took many decisions without consulting the Regency Council; instead, the government of England was increasingly conducted through Somerset's household and there was an increased use of proclamations, rather than Parliament. However, it could be argued that these were necessary given the continual crises that the government faced. Most importantly, Somerset appeared to ignore the advice of other members of the ruling elite, so much so that his close friend and advisor, William Paget, then Secretary and a member of the Privy Council, even wrote to him in critical terms in May 1549:

Source

C **A letter from William Paget to Edward Seymour, Duke of Somerset:**

However it cometh to pass I cannot tell, but of late your Grace is grown in great choleric [angry] fashions, whensoever you are contraried in that which you have conceived in your head. A king which shall give men occasion of discourage to say their opinions frankly receiveth thereby great hurt and peril to his realm. But a subject in great authority, as your Grace is, using such fashion, is like to fall into great danger and peril of his own person, beside that to the commonweal [well-being of the state].

ACTIVITY

1   It was suggested that the date when an account or letter was written is important. Why might Paget be writing in such terms to Somerset in May 1549?

2   What criticisms of Somerset are made by Paget in Source C?

3   What is the purpose of Paget's letter to Somerset?

4   How might this affect its reliability?

Source

D **Only a few weeks later, in July, Paget wrote again to Somerset in the following terms:**

I told your Grace the truth, and was not believed: well, now your Grace seeth it, what seeth your Grace? The King's subjects out of all discipline, out of obedience, caring neither for Protector nor King … Remember what you promised me in the gallery at Westminster before the breath was out of the body of the king that dead is. Remember what you promised immediately after, devising with me concerning the place which you now occupy … and that was to follow mine advice in all your proceedings more than any other man's. Which promise I wish your Grace had kept.

ACTIVITIES

1   It is interesting to consider the tone of Paget's second letter to Somerset (Source D). This can perhaps be best done by reading it out aloud. What is the tone of the letter? Why?

2   It would also be worthwhile to compare the tone of Source D with that of Source C. In what ways are they different? Why?

3   What has happened between Paget's previous letter to Somerset (Source C) and this letter (Source D) which causes him to say the 'King's subjects out of all discipline, out of obedience'?

4   What is the purpose of Source D?

5   According to Source D, what had Somerset promised Paget?

6   How might this affect the reliability of Paget's comments?

2 How stable and well served was the monarchy in this period?

Although many historians have argued that Edward was a sickly child, this is not true. It was only in the early months of 1553 that his health began to decline. The Succession Acts stated that the throne should pass to Mary, his half-sister. But once again, historians disagree about the driving force behind the attempts to prevent her from gaining the throne. Most accounts suggest that it was the Duke of Northumberland who wanted to alter the succession in order to preserve his own power. He had arranged the marriage of his son to Lady Jane Grey, who was proclaimed queen a few days after Edward died on 6 July 1553. Other historians have argued that it was Edward who was behind the **devise** issued in 1553. This declared both Mary and Elizabeth illegitimate and named the male descendants of Lady Jane Grey as heirs. It was argued that Edward did this in order to preserve Protestantism by preventing the Catholic Mary from inheriting the throne. When Edward died, Jane was proclaimed queen and Mary Tudor was informed in the following letter:

devise

In a monarch's will, a clause that deals with the question of who will succeed to the throne.

Source

 E A letter from the Privy Council to Mary Tudor, 9 July 1553.

We advise you that our Sovereign Lady Queen Jane is possessed of the crown, not only by good order of old ancient records of this realm, but also by the late King Edward's letters signed with his own hand and sealed with the Great Seal of England, with nobles, councillors and judges agreeing to these letters. We must remind you that owing to the divorce between King Henry VIII and your mother, in accordance with the law of God and confirmed by acts of parliament (1534, 1537), you are illegitimate and unable to inherit the crown.

ACTIVITY

1   According to the letter from the Privy Council, Source E, what was the basis of Queen Jane's claim to the throne? Why might they have listed so many reasons why Mary was unable to inherit the throne?

2   Why might the letter mention that nobles, councillors and judges had agreed to these letters?

3   What was the purpose of the letter? How might this affect its reliability?

Mary did not accept the situation and as a result England came close to civil war. Northumberland had failed to arrest Mary before Edward died and she had been able to flee to East Anglia, where she was able to raise a large force. Northumberland also attempted to raise an army to capture her, but as it approached Mary's force at Framlingham Castle, many deserted and Northumberland was forced to surrender. Jane's reign had lasted just nine days. Mary was now queen and legitimacy triumphed.

The events of 1553 had shown that legitimacy, rather than religion, should determine the succession and that the rightful ruler was preferable to a usurper.

Source

(F) *To win the throne, Mary relied on a small group of Catholic gentry supporters, but the secret of her success was a much wider appeal to legitimacy and a careful avoidance of religious issues during the course of the crisis itself.*

D. MacCulloch (1990) *The Later Reformation in England 1547–1603.* Macmillan.

ACTIVITY

How far does MacCulloch's view about the reasons for Mary's success in Source F agree with your own knowledge of events?

Read some other historians' writing to increase your understanding of this issue.

Figure 2.4   Queen Mary I, shortly before her marriage to Philip of Spain.

2 How stable and well served was the monarchy in this period?

How serious a threat to the power of the monarchy was a female ruler?

The accession of a female ruler raised many issues in sixteenth-century society. The only other occasion when England had been ruled by a female was in the twelfth century. Then, it had resulted in civil war as many people refused to accept Matilda as queen and backed Stephen instead. There were fears that this would be repeated as Mary would be unable to control the factions within the country, which were made worse by the religious divisions. It was also expected that a ruler would lead the army into battle and it was argued that Mary would be unable to fulfil this role. Most controversially, it was expected that Mary would marry; the problem was who. In the sixteenth century a husband made the decisions, even if his wife was queen! If Mary married an Englishman, a noble family would be placed in a dominant position and control patronage, but if she married a foreigner, the country would face foreign domination.

These latter fears were soon realised when it was announced in November 1554 that Mary was to marry Philip of Spain. Although as the most powerful ruler in Europe, Philip would be able to protect Mary, there were fears that England would be used by Spain and dragged into conflicts that did not benefit England. It is therefore not surprising that the announcement of the marriage resulted in rebellion (see Chapter 5, pages 138–139). However, with the defeat of rebellion Mary would not face other challenges to her position, and it can be argued that it was Mary herself, with a speech at Guildhall, who did much to rally the City and defeat Wyatt.

Once it was clear that Mary was not going to have children, despite her two phantom pregnancies in 1554 and 1557, she reluctantly recognised her half-sister, Elizabeth, as her heir. Mary insisted that Elizabeth should keep England Catholic, and although Elizabeth never agreed to this, when Mary died in November 1558, the throne passed unchallenged to Elizabeth.

How serious a threat to the monarchy were the issues of marriage and succession?

Elizabeth was aware that, as a female ruler, she was in a much weaker position than a man would have been. There was also the practical question of whether a woman could be head of the Church, as there was no scriptural authority for a woman to make doctrinal decisions. As Mary appeared to have proved, there were doubts whether a female ruler had the authority to impose her will. It is therefore not surprising that most people expected Elizabeth to marry. Unlike Mary, she was able to exploit her femininity and was able to woo courtiers like Leicester. She also used it to obtain an extra degree of loyalty from ministers, such as Cecil, who were aware that her gender made her more vulnerable.

Marriage and succession were the two most important policy issues of the early years of Elizabeth's reign. Despite some questions about her legitimacy, from those who did not accept Henry's divorce from Catherine of Aragon, her position as monarch was unchallenged. Her ministers were anxious that she should marry and have an heir, and she faced pressure from both the Privy Council and Parliament on these issues. Although she refused to marry or name a successor, the issue did not go away.

In some ways Elizabeth was fortunate that Mary's husband, Philip of Spain, welcomed her accession. He was still at war with France and was much happier to see Elizabeth queen than Mary Stuart, who was married to the French Dauphin. Marriage and succession were closely linked to foreign policy, as had been the case with Mary. Marriage could also be used as a diplomatic bargaining tool. The same was argued about the naming of a successor.

Many feared that if Elizabeth died childless, the country would be plunged into civil war. However, Elizabeth refused to either marry or name a successor.

Sources

Read the following extracts from speeches by Elizabeth on the issue of marriage and the succession made to her first parliament.

(G) *And to me it shall be a full satisfaction both for the memorial of my name, and for my glory also, if when I shall let my last breath, it be engraven upon my marble tombe, Here Lyeth ELIZABETH, which reigned a virgin and died a virgin.*

(H) *When my sister Mary was Queen, what prayers were made by many to see me placed in her seat … Now then, if the affections of the people grow faint … what may we look for when evil-minded men shall have a great foreign prince appointed the certain successor to the crown? In how great a danger shall I be … when a prince so powerful, so near unto me, shall be declared my successor? Assuredly, if my successor were known to the world, I would never esteem my state to be safe.*

ACTIVITY

What reasons does Elizabeth give in Sources G and H for not marrying or naming a successor?

Elizabeth's views contrasted with those of her advisors, who believed that the naming of a successor was the best guarantee of security. Many suitable husbands were suggested, including Philip of Spain, but as Elizabeth stated, marriage to a heretic was out of the question.

It was Elizabeth's contraction of smallpox in 1562 that brought matters to a head. Her life had been in danger and the security of the realm was seen as threatened. As a result, Parliament raised the issue in 1563 and again in 1566. In 1566 they even tried to link the question of granting a subsidy to Elizabeth's agreement. Elizabeth still refused, and after that date her wishes were reluctantly accepted.

Why did Elizabeth not marry or name a successor?

Reasons to marry	Reasons not to marry	Reasons to name a successor	Reasons not to name a successor
It would provide an heir	She wanted to marry **Robert Dudley**, but could not, therefore she would not marry anyone	Without a clear heir there would be a struggle for the throne	If she named a successor, that person would be the focus of opposition to her
A woman ruling on her own was seen as unnatural; she needed help	She wanted to rule on her own and not share power	If Elizabeth did not name an heir to the throne, Mary Stuart (Queen of Scots) would claim the throne and bring England back to rule by a foreign Catholic power	She would not be bullied into naming a successor; it was a matter of her prerogative
Marriage could be used to get an ally	She felt that being unmarried strengthened her position		Elizabeth was a cautious ruler; she did not want to name a successor and discover she had made a mistake
	She could use her marriage potential by remaining single		There was no suitable candidate

Table 2.1 The many reasons put forward both for and against Elizabeth either marrying or naming a successor.

BIOGRAPHY

Robert Dudley, Earl of Leicester

The son of John Dudley, the Duke of Northumberland, who had been executed in 1553. A firm Protestant, Robert was the favourite of Elizabeth and was appointed to the Privy Council in 1562. He was created Earl of Leicester in 1564. As the Queen's personal favourite, he had considerable access to her, which made him a serious rival to Cecil. There were rumours of him marrying Elizabeth.

ACTIVITY

During the rule of which monarch was the power and authority of the monarchy most seriously threatened? What criteria are you going to use to assess the threat? Try to rank the monarchs according to the threat, giving each a mark out of ten according to how serious the threat was – the higher the mark, the greater the threat.

How far did faction make the monarchy less stable?

The concept of faction is one of the most difficult issues you will have to understand in the course. In very simple terms, faction is when a group of people act together to further their own positions and influence, and undermine the positions and influence of others. These groupings are very loose and should not be confused with the discipline and organisation that surround a modern political party. Factional groups could often be temporary alliances, united only by the desire to remove those who have influence. The historian Eric Ives has defined faction as a group of people who have come together to seek 'objectives that are seen primarily in personal terms'. These groupings were made more confusing by the religious divisions created by the break from Rome and moves away from Catholicism.

In the sixteenth century the royal court was the centre of power and influence. Those looking for promotion needed to attract the attention of the monarch, and this was often done through one of his friends or supporters. Consequently, those looking for promotion gathered around either powerful ministers or nobles and as a result rivalry between the groups developed as they jostled for influence and patronage.

It will be important to consider how far each of these factions was able to dominate the political scene, influence policy and weaken the power of the monarchy in the period. You will need to consider how far the monarch was in control or was dominated by the leading political group.

> ### The main factional struggles in the period 1536–69 centred around the following:
>
> - the Boleyn faction v the Aragonese faction in 1536
> - the Exeter Conspiracy in 1538
> - the reformers, such as Cranmer, v the conservative faction of Gardiner and Norfolk in the 1540s
> - the Seymour dominance at the end of Henry's reign until Somerset's fall in 1549
> - the dominance of the Dudleys from 1551 to 1553
> - the struggle between Paget and Gardiner under Mary Tudor
> - the struggle between Norfolk and Cecil during Elizabeth's reign.

The Boleyn faction v the Aragonese faction

In the 1530s two groups emerged: those who stressed their loyalty to the former queen, Catherine of Aragon and her daughter, Mary Tudor, and those who supported the new queen and wanted to see religious reform (see pages 62–64). It might have been expected that Catherine's death in 1536 would mark the end of the Aragonese faction, but instead it was a spur to action against Anne and her supporters. We have already seen (page 11) that the 1534 Succession Act had removed Mary from the succession, declaring her illegitimate. Their aim was to restore her to the succession. With Catherine dead, they believed that Henry could now do this without implying that his marriage had been legal. They also had other motives. Catherine and her daughter had remained firm Catholics while Anne was identified with religious change, and Catherine's supporters had not forgiven Anne for luring Henry away from Catherine. They set out to bring about Anne's downfall.

They were given a boost when, in January 1534, Anne miscarried. Henry started to have doubts about the legality of his marriage to Anne, and Anne's position was further weakened by the presence of Jane Seymour. The Aragonese faction began to instruct Jane in how to win and keep Henry's affections. This was an obvious threat to the Boleyns' position, and things were made worse by Thomas Cromwell's decision to back the Aragonese faction, having had disputes with the Boleyns about foreign policy.

Cromwell moved quickly. First, Anne's friends were arrested, then Anne herself. They were accused of adultery and finally of conspiring to bring about the death of the King. It was not surprising that they, along with Anne, were found guilty and executed.

How far had faction brought about Anne's downfall? There are certainly grounds for suggesting that Henry played a significant role. He was looking for an opportunity to remove her, convinced that her failure to produce a son was a sign that their marriage was not legal. He was also annoyed by her involvement in politics and religious developments, believing that a wife should keep out of such things. It is therefore possible to argue that Cromwell decided to support the Aragonese faction either because the King requested him to, or because he realised how things were developing and that he must do as the King wished if he was to save his own position.

Having brought down the Boleyns, Cromwell turned on his former allies as he feared they would attack him and bring about a religious reversal. His triumph was secured in the Second Succession Act of 1536, which banned the descendants of both Anne and Catherine from the throne and placed the succession in the hands of the children of Henry's new wife, Jane Seymour.

This was not the end of the story. Having been defeated at court, the Aragonese faction became involved in rebellion to reverse the religious changes and restore Mary to the succession (see Chapter 5, pages 126–130 for more detail). Historians such as Elton have argued that the Pilgrimage of Grace of 1536 was an attempt by a 'court faction to take the battle out of court into the nation, to raise the standard of loyal rebellion as the only way left to them if they were to succeed in reversing the defeats suffered at court and in Parliament, and in forcing the King to change his policy'.

What evidence is there that the Pilgrimage of Grace was due to faction?

- the demands of the Pilgrims called for the restoration of Mary to the succession
- the demands specifically attacked the rule of Cromwell and his associates
- the leaders of the rising, Darcy, Constable and Hussey, had been involved in opposition since at least 1533
- they had been plotting with the Imperial ambassador for a number of years
- the rising was well organised, suggesting that it was not a spontaneous reaction to the dissolution of the smaller monasteries.

If this interpretation is correct, Henry's position was seriously threatened by faction as the scale of the rising was far greater than any army Henry could raise, forcing him into negotiations and compromise. It was only in the early months of 1537 that Henry was able to reassert his authority and remove the ringleaders.

It might be argued that the rising weakened Cromwell's position as the King saw how unpopular his minister was, but this is not convincing as Cromwell continued to rise in power and favour until Henry's disastrous marriage to Anne of Cleves in 1540. It was this and its exploitation by his opponents that led to Cromwell's fall (see page 16).

The Exeter Conspiracy

In many ways this conspiracy was a continuation of the struggle that the Pilgrimage of Grace had revealed. As with the Pilgrimage, the Exeter conspiracy was alleged to want to restore Catholicism, but also to overthrow Henry. According to the plot, Henry Courtenay, the Marquis of Exeter, was to have conspired with Lord Montague and his brothers, Geoffrey and Reginald Pole. This was made more dangerous because the Courtenays and the Poles were both Yorkists with a claim to the throne.

Courtenay and Montague were executed, but most notoriously so was the elderly Countess of Salisbury, whose only crime was being the niece of Edward IV and Richard III.

Evidence does not support the idea of a conspiracy, but suggests that it was the work of Cromwell, who found the discovery of a threat to the King and government an ideal way to secure his position after 1536.

ACTIVITY

Read the following passage from the interrogation of John Collins, a servant of lord Montague, in 1538.

The said Collins says that he heard Lord Montague much praise the learning of Cardinal Pole. He further says that he heard Lord Montague say that knaves rule about the king and he trusted that one day the world would amend and that honest men would rule about the king. He heard Lord Montague say that he trusted to see the abbeys up again and say that Cardinal Pole should marry the Lady Mary and that she should have title to the Crown.

1 What accusations are made by Collins?

2 How convincing is this as evidence that there was a conspiracy?

3 Why might the accusations made by Collins be unreliable?

The reformers v the conservative faction in the 1540s

With the fall of Cromwell in 1540, Henry decided not to appoint another chief minister. The period saw an increasing struggle between the conservative and reform factions, which some historians have seen as a sign of weak royal power, particularly with Henry's declining health. However, others have argued that Henry was always in control and manipulated the struggle to maintain his power.

Conservative faction	Reform faction
Accepted Henry as head of the Church, but did not want changes in doctrine	Accepted Henry as head of the Church, but did want the introduction of Protestant doctrine
Leader was Duke of Norfolk and members included Stephen Gardiner (Bishop of Winchester)	Leaders were Edward Seymour (became Duke of Somerset) and Archbishop Cranmer
Supported the Six Articles Pleased with the removal of Cromwell Pleased when Henry married Catherine Howard, Norfolk's niece Plotted against Cranmer (1543) Plotted against Catherine Parr (1544)	Involved in the foreign wars and success in Scotland Pleased when Catherine Howard fell Associated with Catherine Parr Plotted against Gardiner (1544) Had Norfolk arrested (1546)

Table 2.2   The main elements of the struggle between the reformers and the conservatives.

ACTIVITY
Study Table 2.2. Which group appears to be victorious in the struggle? What evidence is there to support your view?

Table 2.2 seems to suggest that the factional groups were able to influence the King, yet Henry was well aware of many of the intrigues and some have even argued that he encouraged them, as he enjoyed watching noblemen and councillors fighting for domination. It also allowed Henry to maintain control, as neither group was able to dominate and the final decision was always his.

In 1540 it did appear as if the conservative faction had won. They had removed Cromwell (see pages 45–48), had the conservative Six Articles passed (see page 65) and arranged the marriage of Norfolk's niece, Catherine Howard, to Henry. Yet this was all short-lived. The first disaster was the fall of Catherine Howard. The reform faction was able to present the King with compelling evidence of her unfaithfulness. As a result she was executed, along with those accused of adultery, and Norfolk, although he escaped with his life, lost considerable influence.

The conservative faction tried to strike back by accusing Cranmer of heresy. Henry agreed to look into the accusations, but appointed Cranmer to head the enquiry! Henry then married Catherine Parr, a Protestant sympathiser who was close to Seymour. The conservative faction then accused members of her household and by implication the queen, of heresy. This incident perhaps provides the clearest example of Henry manipulating and even enjoying the factional struggle, rather than being manipulated by it. Henry allowed Catherine to be taken to the Tower to be questioned. It appears that she was told about the charges and was allowed to see her husband, where he accepted her promise to follow his religious views. However, Henry did not tell her opponents of this, so when they arrived to arrest her they were greeted with abuse from Henry for trying to carry out a treasonous act. Henry had shown a willingness to allow his wife to suffer, simply to show that he was in control. Most importantly, it was a clear signal to both sides that he was still in control of policy.

This event was followed by the triumph of the reformers. First they were able to remove Gardiner. He was accused of supporting the reinstatement of papal authority and was lucky to avoid the Tower. Doubts still surrounded him as he had been involved in the plot against the Queen, and finally the reformers were able to argue that he was refusing to grant some of his lands to the King. Even though this accusation was false, it was enough to see his removal. Meanwhile, reformers were dominating court, particularly with the appointment of Anthony Denny (see page 30) as Chief Gentleman of the King's Privy Chamber, which allowed him to control access to the King. At the same time, the reform faction was able to obtain the arrest of Norfolk and his son, the Earl of Surrey. Playing on the King's concerns about the succession, they claimed that Surrey had spoken about his family's claim to the throne and had put part of the royal coat of arms on his family emblem without royal approval. He was executed, but Norfolk survived because Henry died before ordering his death.

ACTIVITY

Consider these two interpretations of the period:

- 'The King's control weakened and left him the victim of rival groups.'

- 'For the most part, Henry knew what was happening and played the groups against each other.'

Which interpretation best describes the events of the 1540s? What is your evidence to support your view?

Faction under Edward VI

It can be argued that factional unrest under Edward had a greater impact than at any other time in the mid-Tudor period. This was particularly true from the late summer of 1549, when serious social unrest engulfed much of the country (see pages 130–135), to 1552, when Dudley emerged triumphant.

Although the reformist faction led by Somerset had triumphed in the last year of Henry's reign, his position was not unchallenged. At the same time, the range and scale of the problems he faced made him even more vulnerable. War with Scotland, financial and economic problems and religious uncertainty all made Somerset's position difficult, but his methods of government alienated many. His personal style of government meant that the Privy Council established by Henry was frequently ignored. This caused resentment among men such as Paget, Dudley and **Wriothesley**, and led to the formation of an anti-Somerset faction. This group had little in common, showing how fluid and flexible faction could be: Wriothesley was a religious conservative, Paget was neutral and Dudley was a reformer.

Wriothesley also had personal reasons to attack Somerset, as he had been removed from the Privy Council in March 1549. As a religious conservative, he would have disliked the changes under Somerset (see Chapter 3, pages 71–81) and so once again faction and religion combined to create instability. Dudley, some historians have argued, was ambitious and looking for an opportunity to replace Somerset, and Paget felt that his advice was being ignored (see page 31). The events of the summer of 1549 would provide these men with the opportunity to act.

BIOGRAPHY

Thomas Wriothesley (pronounced 'Risly')

Born in 1505, Wriothesley entered the service of Wolsey and Cromwell. He was a religious conservative, but gained considerable land and wealth from the dissolution of the monasteries. He became one of the principal secretaries in 1540 and was knighted in 1542. He was appointed Lord Chancellor in 1544. He was one of the executors of Henry's will and was created Earl of Southampton in 1547. Under Somerset he lost his position as Lord Chancellor and was removed from the Privy Council, but he was later readmitted and played a key role in Somerset's downfall.

Source

I The following description of the events of autumn 1549 is taken from from Richard Grafton's *A Chronicle at Large and Meere History of the Affayres of Englande* (1569).

After the unrest was pacified and quieted, many of the Lords of the realm, as well as councillors and others who disliked the government of the Protector, began to withdraw themselves from the Court and resorting to London, fell to secret consultation for the redress of things, but namely for the displacing of the said Lord Protector. Suddenly and why, few knew, every Lord and Councillor went through the City armed and likewise had their servants armed. At last a great assembly of Councillors was held at the Earl of Warwick's lodgings, where all the confederates in this matter came armed and finally concluded to take the Tower of London.

The Lord Protector hearing of the manner of the assembly of this council and the taking of the Tower which seemed to him very strange and doubtful, did presently the said night move from Hampton Court taking the King with him to Windsor Castle and there began to fortify the same.

ACTIVITY

Read Source I.

1 Who does Grafton blame for the problems of autumn 1549?

2 What is his evidence to support his view?

3 How far does this agree with your own knowledge of events?

Fearing for his position, Somerset issued a proclamation on 5 October, calling loyal subjects to Hampton Court to defend him and the King against his enemies. This forced his opponents to act and Somerset was removed. Although Dudley emerged in charge, his position was not secure, as the religiously conservative members of the faction did not trust him and were prepared to remove him because of his friendship with Somerset. Consequently, Dudley was forced to turn on his former allies in order to save himself, and by February 1550 the conservative members of the faction were removed from office as Dudley was able to win over Lord Russell and Lord St John. Dudley now had to ally himself with the more religiously radical elements on the Council, with all the implications for religious change that this would bring (see Chapter 3).

> ## *ACTIVITY*
>
> Points for discussion:
>
> 1   How strong is the evidence that Dudley was trying to gain power for himself?
>
> 2   Why was Somerset foolish in summoning the peasantry to his aid in October 1549?
>
> 3   Which individuals were the most important in determining the outcome of events between October 1549 and February 1550? Explain your answer.

Faction under Mary

Critics of Mary's government have argued that her Privy Council was too large and faction-ridden for government to function effectively. This interpretation is supported by the lack of formal council discussion about her decision to marry Philip of Spain. However, this view is balanced by the fact that routine administration was effective. Mary did keep some councillors who had served Edward and were willing to show her loyalty. They included Paget, but she also added men such as Stephen Gardiner, who had been released from the Tower. At the same time there was a group, known as the 'Kenninghall faction', who had helped her gain the throne and now became Privy Councillors as a reward for their loyalty.

Such a large group would have made the council unwieldy, but it was rare for all members to attend and the average size of gatherings was similar to what it had been during Northumberland's rule. Three developments helped this process:

- in 1554 the councillors established a system of committees which excluded the more casual councillors
- in 1555, Philip helped to establish an 'inner council' of nine trustworthy men
- when Philip left England in 1555 and Gardiner died, Paget was able to dominate and complete the reforms, establishing a conciliar form of government.

There were times when factional rivalries did impact on policies, most notably in the friction between Gardiner and Paget. Some have argued that the establishment of the committee system in 1554 may have been Paget's attempt to stop Gardiner from controlling the whole council. Most obviously, Gardiner's attempts to revive the heresy laws in 1554 were blocked when Paget urged the Lords to reject his proposals. This rivalry became more apparent when a similar bill, supported by Paget, was passed a few months later.

Therefore, despite concerns that the size of the council and conflicts between individuals would result in conflict and a paralysis in government, there is little evidence to support this view. There were disputes over specific issues, but for much of the time the council was able to put rivalry aside.

Cecil v Dudley and Norfolk

Historians used to explain Elizabethan politics in terms of factions and the struggles between the various groups. Although this view has changed in recent years, the role of Cecil in the factional struggles has not. Rather than using faction to promote and secure his own position, there were even occasions when he intervened with the Queen in favour of one of his opponents.

Despite this, Cecil was often the victim of attacks and therefore frequently on the defensive. This is best explained by the fact that he was usually the dominant force who was trying to

stop his opponents from bringing about change. The clearest examples of this both involved Robert Dudley.

On the first occasion, Cecil acted to prevent Dudley's marriage to Elizabeth. Before Dudley's wife had died, Cecil spread a rumour that Dudley was going to murder his wife in order to be free to marry the Queen, and after her 'accidental' death, Cecil spread rumours that Dudley was responsible. As a result, the marriage never took place, since Dudley was seen as an unsuitable husband. Some have argued that as Elizabeth was unable to marry her favourite, she was determined never to marry.

The second event was in 1569, when Dudley combined with the conservative Duke of Norfolk to try to bring down Cecil. In 1568 Norfolk was a supporter of Cecil and a rival of Dudley. It was Cecil's continued monopoly of influence that brought together the unholy alliance of Dudley and Norfolk with other councillors as they tried to end Cecil's domination of court, showing how fluid factional groupings were. There were genuine concerns that Cecil's policy was placing the country in serious danger, and there is certainly some truth in this view. The seizure of the Spanish bullion ships (see page 58) provoked hostility from Spain and led to the seizure of English ships and goods in the Netherlands ports and the banning of all trade with England. Elizabeth retaliated and trade with Spain and the Netherlands stopped. It was not just Dudley and Norfolk who attacked Cecil's policy, but many council members, and for several months they tried to turn the Queen against him.

Although there was a factional element to this crisis, it must be noted that there was a genuine difference in policy between the two groups. However, it is unlikely that Elizabeth would have allowed the anti-Spanish policy to be pursued if she had not known how weak Philip's position was with a rebellion at home and the threat from the Turks in the Mediterranean. Yet this factional conflict did have consequences. In 1569 a rebellion broke out in northern England (see Chapter 5, pages 139–141), and the rebels had certainly been encouraged by the Spanish ambassador. It may also have prompted the Pope to finally issue the Bull of Excommunication which freed Catholics from their loyalty to Elizabeth.

If the conflict was about favour, it was Cecil who emerged victorious. His major opponent, the Duke of Norfolk, was executed in 1572 as a result of his involvement in plots with Mary Queen of Scots. If in 1569 Cecil had appeared to be friendless and virtually isolated, by 1572 he had emerged triumphant. Although the struggle did have an impact on policy, it must also be remembered that there was much co-operation in the governing of the country, suggesting that faction did little to weaken the efficiency of government and the power of the monarch.

ACTIVITY

How convincing is the argument that faction caused instability throughout the period?

In order to reach a conclusion about this question, consider the following points.

- When did faction cause instability?
- How long-lasting was the instability?
- How serious was the instability? Did it prevent government from functioning?
- Were there any periods when the monarch used factional struggles to increase their power?

How well served by ministers was the monarchy in the period 1536–69?

The main focus will be on analysing how far the rule of each of the ministers strengthened or weakened the power of the monarch. The section will centre on the following ministers:

- Cromwell
- Cranmer
- Somerset
- Northumberland
- Pole
- Cecil.

Cromwell

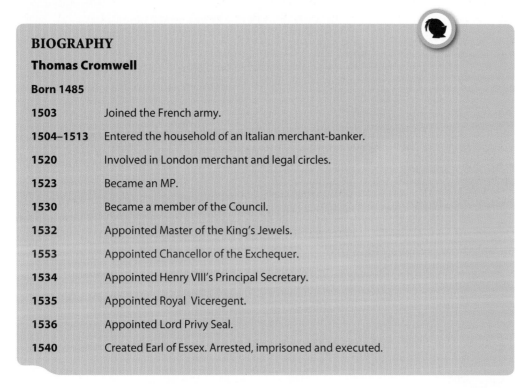

BIOGRAPHY

Thomas Cromwell

Born 1485

1503	Joined the French army.
1504–1513	Entered the household of an Italian merchant-banker.
1520	Involved in London merchant and legal circles.
1523	Became an MP.
1530	Became a member of the Council.
1532	Appointed Master of the King's Jewels.
1553	Appointed Chancellor of the Exchequer.
1534	Appointed Henry VIII's Principal Secretary.
1535	Appointed Royal Viceregent.
1536	Appointed Lord Privy Seal.
1540	Created Earl of Essex. Arrested, imprisoned and executed.

Cromwell was Henry's principal minister from 1532 to 1540. There is much debate about his achievements, but he did bring about many changes to the way England was governed, so much so that Elton argued that they amounted to a 'revolution in government'. However, there is also much debate about his motives. Cardinal Pole described him as 'an agent of Satan sent by the devil to lure King Henry to damnation', and said that he was simply motivated by personal greed. Cromwell, however, claimed that his beliefs and views always took second place to those of the King. Within months of Cromwell's death, Henry was agreeing and historians have suggested that he was the best minister any monarch was fortunate enough to be served by in the sixteenth century. This view appears to be given credence by a brief examination of his achievements set out below.

Figure 2.5 Thomas Cromwell.

- He brought about an administrative revolution in the structure and organisation of central government.
- Financial departments were reorganised.
- The Privy Council was created.
- The role of Parliament was increased.
- The areas and authority of statute law were increased.
- He created the concept of national sovereignty.

- He brought about a revolution in the relationship between Church and state; the independence of the Church was removed.
- Royal authority was extended in the regions; more authority was given to the Council of the North and the government of Wales was reformed.

From this summary, it does appear as if Cromwell achieved a great deal for Henry. He always appeared to put his master's needs first and abandoned his own ideas and policies if they were not favoured by the King, though some have suggested that his loyalty had other motives.

Source

J **Comments said to have been made about Thomas Cromwell by George Paulet, who appeared before a Royal Commission to answer charges of slandering the minister:**

…the King beknaveth him [calls him bad names/swears at him] … twice a week and sometimes knocketh him well about the head; and yet when he hath been well pummelled about the head or shaken up as it were a dog, he will come out into the Great Chamber and shaking off the bush with as merry a countenance as though he might rule the roost.

Commission of Investigation report, 1538.

ACTIVITY

1   What criticisms are made of Cromwell in Source J?

2   What does Source J suggest about the relationship between Henry and Cromwell?

Remember the following points when considering reliability:

- What is the nature of the source?
- Why was the source produced?
- How will this affect the reliability of the source?

Source

K **In 1540 Cromwell was attainted for treason and executed, as described in this extract from the Bill of Attainder of Thomas Cromwell, June 1540. The Bill of Attainder was drawn up by the House of Lords, many of whom were opposed to Cromwell because of his dominance at court and his background.**

Attainder of Thomas Cromwell, Earl of Essex, whom the King has raised from a very base and low degree to the state of an earl and who nevertheless has been the most detestable traitor that has been since the King's reign. He has, of his own authority, set at liberty persons convicted of misprision [erroneous judgement] of treason … and also has, for sums of money, granted licences for the export of money, corn etc. contrary to the King's proclamations; and also, being a detestable heretic, has dispersed into all shires false and erroneous books, many of which were printed beyond the seas, tending to the discredit of the blessed sacrament of the altar and other articles of religion declared by the King by the authority of Parliament.

ACTIVITIES

Before answering these questions, you should look carefully at the language used by the writers of Source K. You should be able to identify words which clearly show their attitude towards Cromwell.

1   What charges are made against Cromwell in the **Bill of Attainder**?

2   What area of activity does most of the Bill focus on? Why might this be the case?

3   What is the purpose of the Bill?

4   How might this affect the reliability of Source K?

5   How does the nature of the Bill affect the reliability of Source K?

Bill of Attainder

A declaration by Parliament that a person was guilty of treason. This would happen without a trial. The declaration also applied to the person's heirs and would mean the loss of the family estate.

Having looked at the list of Cromwell's achievements and the Act of Attainder, you should now consider whether Cromwell was a good servant of the monarch or just a greedy Tudor statesman.

Cranmer

BIOGRAPHY

Thomas Cranmer

1489	Born in Nottinghamshire.
1520s	Studied at Cambridge and was a member of the 'White Horse' Group.
c.1532	Secretly married the niece of a Lutheran Church leader from Nuremberg.
1533	Appointed Archbishop of Canterbury.
1533	Presided over Henry VIII's divorce from Catherine of Aragon.
1534	Declared Henry head of the Church in England.
1536	Prounounced Henry's marriage to Anne Boleyn null and void; presided over Henry's marriage to Jane Seymour.
1539	Opposed the Act of Six Articles, but refused to resign.
1541–47	Leader of the reformist party at court, survived conservative attacks.
1547–53	Played a leading role in the Edwardian Reformation.
1553	Stripped of title of Archbishop of Canterbury.
1554	Arrested and imprisoned for heresy.
1556	Burned at the stake.

Figure 2.6   Thomas Cranmer.

There has been significant debate about Cranmer for over 400 years, with Catholic historians seeing him as failing to save the Church for Rome, while Protestant writers have seen him as establishing the Church of England and as a martyr who was burnt for his beliefs by Mary Tudor.

Of greater interest in recent years has been the debate over how and why Cranmer was able to survive a period which many others, such as Cromwell, did not. He had spent much of his early life at Cambridge University, but came to prominence with his writing in support

2 How stable and well served was the monarchy in this period?

of Henry's divorce from Catherine. With the death of Archbishop Warham, to the surprise of many, Cranmer was made Archbishop of Canterbury in 1533. Henry undoubtedly liked Cranmer, and contemporaries also commented on the pleasure of his company. The King trusted him, particularly after his handling of the divorce, and was certain that he did not have his own policy agenda, as Cromwell had. In simple terms, he was a 'yes' man who accepted Henry's decisions and did his best to put them into practice. However, Cranmer also believed that it was his duty to offer the King advice, even when he knew it would not be well received. He argued that the disgrace of Anne Boleyn should not derail the Reformation, pleaded with the King for leniency towards Cromwell and broke the news to Henry about Catherine Howard's adultery. In theological matters, Cranmer explained in detail why Henry's objections to the Bishop's Book were ill founded.

ACTIVITY

The following passage is taken from a letter written by Cranmer to the King about Cromwell.

He that was such a servant, in my judgement, in wisdom, diligence, faithfulness, and experience, as no prince in this realm ever had ... I loved him as my friend, for so I took him to be; but chiefly I loved him for the love which I thought I saw him bear towards your Grace, above all other. But now, if he be a traitor, I am sorry I ever loved him or trusted him, and I am very glad that his treason is discovered in time; but again I am very sorrowful; for who shall your Grace trust hereafter, if you might not trust him? I pray God continually night and day, to send such a councillor in his place whom your Grace may trust, and who for all his qualities can and will serve your Grace like to him.

1 What is Cranmer's view of Cromwell as expressed in the passage? What is your evidence to support this view?

2 What do you think was the purpose of Cranmer's letter? How does this affect its reliability?

3 Why might such a letter be risky for Cranmer? Does this mean his views are more or less likely to be reliable?

If Cranmer was a Lutheran, as many believe, why did he survive when others such as Cromwell fell because of their heretical beliefs? The likely answer to this also explains his skill: he was able to separate his own beliefs from the policy he was asked to follow. He passed judgements of heresy on people whose beliefs were no different from his own!

For Henry, Cranmer's greatest achievement was in overseeing the divorce from Catherine, but Cranmer did influence the direction of the Reformation. He supported Cromwell's attempts to move the country in a more Protestant direction in the years after 1536, and when he was given a similar opportunity after 1543 he followed a similar policy. Having survived attempts by the conservative faction to remove him (see pages 39–41), he was able to bring in his Litany and the King's Prymer. After Henry's death, Cranmer produced the Book of Homilies, or model sermons, followed by his Prayer Books of 1549 and 1552 (see Chapter 3, pages 74–75).

Somerset

BIOGRAPHY

Edward Seymour, Duke of Somerset

Born **c.1506**

1537	Appointed to Privy Council.
1541	Created Earl of Hertford.
1547	Created Duke of Somerset and Lord Protector.
1549	Fall of Somerset.
1552	Executed.

There is much debate about Somerset. Some historians describe him as the 'good duke' who was concerned for the poor, while to others he was a typical Tudor statesman, greedy and out to improve his own position. When in power he certainly ensured that he obtained large amounts of wealth through the sale of Chantry lands and rewarded his supporters well. He established an Enclosure Commission in 1548 to look into the complaints of the peasantry. This appeared to encourage the peasants to take the law into their own hands, with the result that by the summer of 1549 the country appeared to be drifting towards a major crisis. There were rebellions in 25 counties and Somerset appeared unable to control the situation. It was this failure that led ultimately to his fall from power in the autumn of 1549. He was abandoned by other members of the council, who blamed him for failing to prevent the unrest. On the other hand, John Dudley, who had defeated the rebels in East Anglia, had gained in popularity and was able to engineer Somerset's arrest.

Source

(L) *Somerset was the victim of a political coup in October 1549. The new regime blamed him for what had gone wrong in 1549, especially the bungled handling of the revolts which had allowed them to go on for so long. In fact, the policy which Somerset's government had adopted had been the work of the whole Council. Nevertheless, it is true that on occasion Somerset had gone against the advice of his councillors, sometimes with disastrous consequences. An example was the enclosure commissions of 1548 and 1549 which, as some councillors had predicted, caused rather than stopped the revolts.*

M.L. Bush (1975) *The Government Policy of Protector Somerset*. McGill-Queens University Press.

ACTIVITY

1   What is Bush's view in Source L about why Somerset fell from power?

2   How far does Bush blame Somerset for the problems in dealing with the unrest in 1549?

3   How accurate is Bush's explanation for the fall of Somerset?

Source

 Richard Grafton, a well-informed Londoner, writing in 1568 about the events of 1549.

After the rebellions were crushed, many of the lords and councillors secretly plotted to overthrow the Lord Protector. Each lord and councillor went through London armed, and had their servants likewise armed. They published a proclamation against him containing the following charges. First, that through his malicious and evil government, the Lord Protector had caused all the recent unrest in the country. Second, he was ambitious and sought his own glory, as appeared by his lavish buildings. Third, that he ignored the advice of the councillors. Fourth, that he told untruths about the council to the King.

ACTIVITY

1   What reasons did the proclamation against Somerset (described in Source M) give for his removal?

2   Look carefully at the language used in the proclamation. What words are used to describe Somerset's government and personality? Why would such words and phrases be used?

3   What do you think was the purpose of the proclamation?

4   How might this affect the reliability of the proclamation?

Although Somerset was arrested in 1549, he was released in 1550 and was able to rejoin the Privy Council. However, the following year he was accused of plotting against the Privy Council in order to regain power, and was arrested and executed in 1552.

Source

N Francis Bourgoyne, who was based in London, relates the events leading to the execution of Somerset, in a letter to the Protestant theologian John Calvin, 22 January 1552.

Somerset was the head of a conspiracy against the whole Council, and more particularly against the Duke of Northumberland, whom Somerset pursued with a deadly hatred, since Northumberland had been foremost among those who deprived him of the rank of Lord Protector. Somerset obtained some supporters from among the Council itself. They agreed that Northumberland should be murdered and they should take over the government of the kingdom. Somerset should lead the government, or even be restored to the office of Protector.

Having looked at the fall and execution of Somerset, you should now decide whether Somerset was more interested in personal wealth than in serving the King.

Northumberland

BIOGRAPHY

John Dudley, Duke of Northumberland

Born in 1504, Dudley held various posts under Henry VIII. In 1542 he became Viscount Lisle, and during the 1540s developed a military reputation with victories on land and sea against the French and Scots. On Henry's death in 1547 he became Earl of Warwick and Lord Great Chamberlain. In 1549 he crushed Kett's Rebellion. In October 1549 he was involved in the removal of Somerset, and in January 1550 became Lord President of the Council. In October 1551 he was created Duke of Northumberland. In 1553 he attempted to change the succession and was executed following the failure of the Lady Jane Grey affair.

As with Somerset, there is much debate about Northumberland. His reputation was low. He was seen to have conspired with the conservative group on the Council to remove Somerset, and then turned on them to increase his own power. Having brought Somerset back into the Council, he had him executed. Finally he conspired against Mary, then on the scaffold renounced his Protestantism in a vain attempt to save his life. More recent work has focused on the positive aspects of his rule, arguing that it restored stability and order after the rebellions and was welcomed by property-holders and landowners. His action against the conservative councillors was forced on him to save his own position before they turned on him, and Somerset was executed because he tried to regain his former position. Although it is more difficult to defend Northumberland's actions in 1553, it has been suggested that he was only carrying out the young King's wishes.

Source

Ⓞ Robert Wingfield, a Suffolk gentleman and Catholic supporter of Queen Mary, assesses Northumberland's role in the attempt to change the succession, writing in 'The Life of Queen Mary', 1553.

The Duke of Northumberland was an ambitious man. After a notable victory outside Norwich in 1549 against the peasants, who had been stirred up against the better sort by idle men, Northumberland sought to control both the King and the kingdom. In 1553 the King showed signs of imminent death. He dared not make any protests, but fell in with the Duke's wishes to alter the succession. The dying King spoke to the nobles and lawyers: 'It is our resolve, with the agreement of our noblemen, to appoint as our heir our dear cousin Jane. For if our sister Mary were to be queen, all would be over for the religion we have established.'

ACTIVITY

Read Source O.

1   Who does Wingfield believe was behind the plot to alter the succession in 1553?

2   What is Wingfield's view of Northumberland?

3   Why might Wingfield's view of Northumberland be unreliable?

4   What reason does Wingfield give for the attempt to alter the succession? Why might he portray it in these terms? How reliable is his view?

Although Wingfield argues that the preservation of the Protestant religion was the most important reason for the attempt to alter the succession, he also suggests that ambition played a role. This view is supported by the fact that Northumberland had married his son, Guildford, to Jane Grey, which allowed him to continue to dominate politics even after the death of Edward. This would also suggest that Northumberland was the driving force behind the plot. However, the failure of the plot suggests that the driving force behind it might have been the young King Edward, rather than the ambitious Duke. Northumberland was an experienced soldier and would have ensured that Mary was captured before Edward died.

Source

 A modern historian writes about the attempts to alter the succession.

Edward VI contracted tuberculosis in 1553, and with his heir under the terms of his father's will well known to be a Catholic, disaster loomed for the Protestant cause. Between them, the young king and Northumberland determined to alter the succession to secure Protestantism. That they did not succeed is one of the great surprises of sixteenth-century English politics.

D. MacCulloch (1990) *The Later Reformation in England 1547–1603*. Macmillan.

ACTIVITY

1   What is MacCulloch's view about the cause of the attempt to alter the succession in 1553?

2   Who does MacCulloch believe was behind the plot?

Having looked in detail at the events of 1553, you should now consider whether Northumberland was a power-hungry politician or an able statesman who acted in the interests of the young King.

Pole

> **BIOGRAPHY**
>
> **Cardinal Pole**
>
> **1500**   Birth of Pole (his mother was Countess of Salisbury).
>
> **1515**   Educated at Oxford University.
>
> **1530**   Refused to be Archbishop of York.
>
> **1531**   Opposed Henry's divorce.
>
> **1532**   Went abroad to study.
>
> **1536**   Attacked Henry's supremacy.
>
> **1537**   Made a cardinal and **papal legate** to England.
>
> **1538**   Brother executed by Henry.
>
> **1541**   Mother executed.
>
> **1554**   Pole returned to England.
>
> **1555**   Pole appointed Archbishop of Canterbury.
>
> **1558**   Death of Pole.

papal legate
An envoy of the Pope. Pole was the Pope's representative in England.

Pole's return to England in 1554 marked a further move in the restoration of Catholicism. Having been abroad for over 20 years, he was somewhat out of touch with political developments in England. Pole was responsible for the reconciliation of England with Rome, but this came at a price: Mary had to compromise over the return of former monastic lands, so there could not be a full-scale restoration of monasticism in England (see Chapter 3).

There was little doubt that Pole's aims were similar to Mary's. Both wanted to eradicate Protestantism, both wanted to resolve the financial position of the Church and ensure that there was better clerical education and discipline. On Gardiner's death in 1555, Pole became archbishop of Canterbury. This gave him the opportunity to increase the level of persecution, resulting in 274 executions in the last three years of Mary's reign, though the impact of the persecutions is now considered to have been minimal (see Chapter 3, pages 85–88). In his attempts to restore church finance, Pole was slightly more successful and this was essential if sufficient resources were to be available to reorganise the Church. He was able to establish seminaries to train priests in every diocese, but a shortage of money meant that the only one was at York. Consequently, many priests remained uneducated and lacking in zeal, so that the changes had limited impact.

Pole was also unable to mount a propaganda campaign to counter the large number of Protestant pamphlets that were starting to appear. He failed to inspire the clergy and bishops to greater efforts and his task was not helped by the death of Pope Julius III in 1555. The new Pope, Paul IV, disliked Pole: he stripped him of his title of legate and ordered him back to Rome. Pole refused to go, but the papacy refused to recognise his authority, which meant he could no longer appoint bishops. As a result, by 1558 seven dioceses lacked bishops. Many must have questioned the wisdom of returning to Rome.

Although Pole had pursued the policies Mary wanted, he had done little to win over the majority of the population. It is almost symbolic of his ultimate failure that he died on the same day as Mary.

Cecil

BIOGRAPHY

William Cecil

1520	Born in Lincolnshire, the son of a family of minor gentry.
1543	Became an MP.
1550	Appointed Surveyor of Elizabeth's Estates.
1550–53	Secretary of State under Northumberland.
1553	Fell from power under Mary.
1558	Elizabeth appointed him Secretary of State.
1561	Appointed Master of the Court of Wards and Liveries.
1568	Leicester and Norfolk plotted to reduce his power.

Elizabeth relied heavily on William Cecil and took his advice on many issues. It was his advice she listened to in 1560, both over sending an expedition to Scotland and not marrying Robert Dudley.

Source

Q **The following description of William Cecil was written by the Spanish ambassador to the King of Spain.**

The principal person in the Council at present is William Cecil, now Lord Burghley. He is a man of mean sort, but very astute, false, lying, and full of artifice. He is a great heretic and such a clownish Englishman as to believe that all the Christian princes joined together are not able to injure the sovereign of his country. By means of his vigilance and craftiness, together with his utter unscrupulousness of word and deed, he thinks to outwit the ministers of other princes.

ACTIVITY

1   What is the ambassador's view of Cecil?

2   Why might he have this view?

3   Why might his view be unreliable? Think about the origin and purpose of Source Q.

Most historians agree that Cecil was the greatest of Elizabeth's ministers; he worked with her for most of his reign, demonstrating a talent for administration. It was Cecil who promoted policies of moderation, particularly in religion, but they brought him into conflict with Leicester, who wanted a more openly anti-Catholic policy (see page 36).

Figure 2.7   William Cecil, Elizabeth's principal secretary of state.

Source

Ⓡ **Read the following passage written by William Cecil to his son, Robert, just before William's death. It outlines how he saw his relationship with Elizabeth.**

I do hold, and always will, this course in such matters as I differ in opinion from Her Majesty: as long as I may be allowed to give advice I will not change my opinion, but as a servant I will obey Her Majesty's commandment, presuming that she being God's chief minister here, it shall be God's will to have her commandment obeyed.

ACTIVITY

1   What advice does William Cecil give to his son?

2   Using your own knowledge, how far do you agree that William Cecil followed the advice he gave his son and was a faithful servant to the Queen in the period 1558–69?

How well did Cecil serve the monarchy?

He persuaded Elizabeth to aid the Scottish rebels in 1560 (see below). This secured the success of the Reformation in Scotland and drove the French out, helping to undermine the 'auld alliance' between France and Scotland and secure England's northern frontier.

- In 1568 he persuaded Elizabeth to seize Spanish treasure ships while they sheltered in English ports. He argued that the money did not belong to the Spanish until it reached the Netherlands and therefore still belonged to the Genoese bankers; Elizabeth was free to borrow it.
- Contemporaries commented on how much work he did.
- He drafted Elizabeth's correspondence with foreign ambassadors and agents.
- He was her main advisor in foreign affairs.
- He managed the business of the Houses of Parliament.
- He followed a cautious economic policy, which would enable England to withstand the cost of war later in Elizabeth's reign.
- He helped to create an effective intelligence service at home and overseas.
- He created an excellent propaganda system which helped secure the throne for Elizabeth and acceptance of the Religious Settlement (see pages 90–91).

Nevertheless, the picture of the honest servant who advised the Queen has been challenged, and it has been suggested that he was the 'power behind the throne'. Three incidents in the early years have been used to support this interpretation. First, letters have been found in which he told English ambassadors abroad what to write to the Queen so that she received the version of events that he wanted, and secondly, reinterpretation of the agitation behind the issue of succession in Parliament in 1563 and 1566 makes it clear that Cecil was trying to pressurise Elizabeth into accepting his views. The third and clearest example of Cecil imposing his will on the Queen was in 1559, when he conspired with fellow councillors to persuade her to accept armed intervention in Scotland to support Protestantism against Mary of Guise, the Regent, even though Elizabeth had stated that she was opposed to such a policy.

ACTIVITY

Read the following extract from a modern historian about William Cecil.

His labour and care were so incessant and his study so great as, in cases of necessity, he turned neither for meat, sleep or rest, till his business was brought to some end. This industry caused all his friends to pity him and his very servants to admire him.

A.G.R. Smith (1990) *The 'Anonymous Life' of William Cecil, Lord Burghley.*

1   What impression does the extract give of Cecil?

2   Using your own knowledge, would you agree with the assessment?

Reaching judgements

In the examination it is important to reach a judgement in all the questions you answer. The exercises below are designed to help you develop this important skill.

Now that you have examined the role of the ministers in the period 1536–69, you should think about the following:

- What criteria are you going to use to judge the service the ministers gave?
- Which minister best served the Tudor monarchy? Why do you think this?
- Which minister was most interested in acquiring personal wealth? What is your evidence?

Overall, do you think the Tudor monarchs were well served by their ministers in this period? To help you answer this question, you might draw up a chart similar to the one below.

Minister	Evidence that they served the monarchy well	Evidence that they did not serve the monarchy well
Cromwell		
Cranmer		
Somerset		
Northumberland		
Pole		
Cecil		

You could consider giving each minister a mark out of ten, according to how well they served the monarch, and explaining why you have given them this mark.

Did the challenges you have studied cause a political crisis?

Arguments that they did:

- Henry's last years were dominated by factional struggle and royal authority was weakened.
- Somerset seized power through a political coup and the manipulation of Henry's will.
- Somerset was able to divert government through his own household and his use of proclamations.
- Somerset's government lost the support of the political elites, shown in his failure to manage the rebellions of 1549.
- The fall of Somerset led to an autumn of instability.
- Northumberland was able to control the King through the Privy Council.
- The Lady Jane Grey affair led to rival armies being raised.
- Wyatt's Rebellion was a serious challenge to Mary.

Arguments that they did not:

- The permanent machinery of state always functioned.
- The ruling elites supported the legitimate monarch.

2 How stable and well served was the monarchy in this period?

■ The factional rivalry was no greater than it had been under either Henry VII or in the early years of Henry VIII.

■ The Crown passed to Henry's children, as stipulated in the Third Succession Act and his will.

■ The crisis of October 1549 when Somerset tried to seize Edward and was subsequently overthrown was short-lived.

■ The attempt to place Lady Jane Grey on the throne lasted only nine days, and when Northumberland left London the support of the political elite swung behind Mary.

■ Administration continued even when leadership was weak.

■ The Crown passed peacefully from Henry VIII to Edward VI.

■ Northumberland was an able politician who brought stability and reform.

■ The Crown passed peacefully from Mary to Elizabeth.

ACTIVITY

Having studied the challenges of the period, you should be able to form your own view of how stable and well served the monarchy was. Draw up a chart like the one below. Consider the following periods and give each one a mark out of ten for how stable it was.

Date	Evidence of stability	Evidence of a crisis	Mark/10	Explanation
1530s				
1540–47				
1547–50				
1550–53				
1554–58				
1558–69				

You should also consider what type of challenge posed the greatest threat to the monarchy.

How significant were the religious changes of the period?

> It is important to remember that this is a source paper. In this section you will be encouraged to develop the skills needed to compare sources. The emphasis will be on comparing the content and **provenance** of sources in order to reach a judgement about their usefulness in addressing the issue raised.
>
> How far did the changes between 1536 and 1547 make England a more Protestant country?
>
> What were the major religious changes in the period?
>
> - The Dissolution of the Monasteries, 1536 and 1539
> - The Ten Articles, 1536
> - Royal Injunction, 1536
> - The Bishop's Book, 1537
> - Royal Injunctions, 1538
> - The Great Bible, 1539
> - The Six Articles, 1539
> - The King's Book, 1543
> - The English Litany.
>
> In order to answer this question it is easier to divide the period into two parts: the period from 1536 to the start of 1540, and then from 1540 to 1547. However, you should consider not only the legal changes to religious practices, but also their impact on ordinary people in the towns and villages.

What was the religious situation in 1536?

Henry VIII had broken from the Catholic Church in 1533. This had been necessary in order to obtain a divorce from his first wife, Catherine of Aragon. Henry was impatient to remarry as his mistress, Anne Boleyn, was pregnant and he needed to ensure that the child was legitimate, particularly if it was a boy, as he wanted a male heir (see Chapter 1). It is therefore important to be clear that the break with the Catholic Church was mainly for political, rather than religious reasons.

Although the break removed the Pope as head of the Church in England, it did not mean that Henry was about to embark on a Protestant Reformation (see Chapter 1, pages 11–14). In fact, events and Henry's own religious beliefs suggest that this was far from his thoughts. Henry had written a book attacking **Martin Luther** and had received the title 'defender of the faith' from the Pope in 1521. He had also spent a long time trying to persuade and pressurise the Pope into granting his divorce, again suggesting that he was reluctant to break from the papacy.

It used to be thought that Henry was pushed into a Protestant Reformation because of the **anti-clerical** feeling of the country. However, historians such as Christopher Haigh and J.J. Scarisbrick have done much to discredit this view, showing that the Catholic Church

provenance
The origin of a source: you should consider issues such as author, date, purpose, audience, tone and the typicality of the view expressed.

anti-clerical
Opposed to the influence or power of the Church.

Church calendar
The yearly cycle of religious festivals.

Hunne Case, 1514
Hunne was a London merchant who refused to pay the required fees to the Church on the death of his son. He was later found murdered in a Church prison, and although no member of the clergy was convicted of his murder, it was generally believed that a clergyman had killed him. The case was used by many historians as an example of Church corruption, but more recently historians have seen the incident as an exception.

Rogationtide
A religious festival where crops were blessed and prayers were said for the harvest.

Church ales
Fundraising banquets that provided the Church with most of its income.

Holy Days

Annual saints' days, which were holidays from work. There were often religious ceremonies and processions on these days. Protestants wanted to end them as they believed they encouraged laziness.

primers

Small books that set out basic religious beliefs, much like a textbook.

books of hours

Books that contained prayers to be said at certain times during the day.

Act of Supremacy, 1534

This Act recognised Henry as head of the Church. It also gave him power over its doctrine and beliefs, and would allow him to make changes in these areas.

Act in Restraint of Appeals, 1533

This Act prevented people in England appealing to the Pope on religious issues. The highest court of appeal would now be in England, which was now free from foreign intervention, hence the statement that England was an 'empire'.

Dissolution of the Smaller Monasteries

This Act closed down all monasteries with an income of less than £200 per year, resulting in the closure of about 285 monasteries out of 850.

was popular on the 'eve of the Reformation' and satisfied the spiritual needs of the population. There were few complaints about the condition of the Church and those there were, such as the **Hunne Case**, were exceptions rather than the norm. In the countryside the **Church calendar** coincided with the agricultural cycle, with events such as **Rogationtide** and harvest festival; it also provided a social life through **Church ales** and **Holy Days** which provided peasants with holidays. In the towns, the situation was no different; the needs of an increasingly literate population were met through the printing of books such as **primers** and **books of hours**. This interpretation reinforces the view that the religious changes of Henry's reign were, at least initially, the result of political needs rather than religious ones.

The changes in the period 1529–36 support this interpretation. The various laws passed by Parliament in this period did not change the Catholic doctrine or the ritual of the Church. Instead, the Acts of Parliament focused on changing the legal or jurisdictional situation. The **Act of Supremacy** and the **Act in Restraint of Appeals** removed the Pope as head of the Church and replaced him with the King; they also prevented divorce cases from being heard in Rome. As the Act in Restraint of Appeals stated, 'this realm is an empire', meaning that England was an independent state, free from foreign intervention. These changes would have had little impact on ordinary people.

It is therefore not surprising that there was little opposition to the changes, particularly as the Treason Act provided Henry with the ultimate weapon – death – for those who dared to oppose. This power was vital as Henry had no police force to impose law and order. By using Parliament to pass all of the measures, he had also been able to ensure that most Members of Parliament supported, or at least had approved, the measures, making it harder for them to lead opposition when they returned to their counties.

The only change that would have had any impact on the daily life of the peasantry would have been the **Dissolution of the Smaller Monasteries** in 1536. Although this may appear to be a move towards Protestantism (Lutherans did not see the value of the monastic life and monasteries were also places where prayers for the dead were said), only the smaller monasteries were closed. In fact it was not unusual for monasteries to be closed; Wolsey had closed a number in the 1520s. Therefore it is probably safe to conclude that in 1536 there was no plan for the wholesale suppression of monasteries.

BIOGRAPHY

Martin Luther (1483–1546)

A German monk who, in 1517, nailed to a church door a series of 97 articles, or Theses, criticising the Catholic Church. This led to the start of the Reformation and the establishment of the Lutheran church in parts of Germany. His ideas later spread to Scandinavia and also the Netherlands, which was ruled by Catholic Spain. There were some Lutherans in England, but in 1529 their numbers were insignificant.

How significant were the religious changes of the period 1536–40?

The first significant act was the Dissolution of the Smaller Monasteries in 1536. This followed Cromwell (see Chapter 1) sending his agents to carry out a **visitation** of all monasteries to check on the standards and behaviour of monks and nuns. The agents were well prepared and knew the type of evidence that Cromwell wanted in order to justify the closures.

Sources

A **Richard Layton, one of the two chief inspectors (visitors), writing to Cromwell in December 1535.**

I visited them, and there found two of the said nuns not barren; one of them pregnant by the sub-prior and the other by a serving man. At another priory, where there were four or five nuns with the prioress, one of them had two fair children and another one. At St Andrew's in Northampton the house [i.e. the nunnery] is greatly in debt, the lands sold and the land let out.

B **John Tregonwell to Cromwell, September 1535.**

After my departing from Oxford I went to Godstow where I found all things well and in good order as well in the monastery and also in the convent, except one sister broke her chastity, but for correction and punishment she had been sent to Godstow, where she lives virtuously. From there I went to Eynsham, where the abbot lives a chaste life and supervises well the reparations of his house. I can object to nothing but that he is negligent in overseeing his brethren.

ACTIVITY

Read Sources A and B.

1   What impression of the monasteries does Source A give?

2   What was the purpose of Source A? How might this affect its reliability?

3   Define the following words: priory, convent, chastity, abbot.

4   What impression of the monasteries does Source B give?

5   In what ways is Source B different from Source A?

6   Which source would have pleased Cromwell the most? Why?

7   Why do the sources give different views about the condition of the monasteries?

8   Which source do you think is more trustworthy? Why?

You are now in a position to answer the following question:

9   Compare the two sources as evidence for the condition of monasteries on the eve of the dissolution.

visitation

This was like an inspection. The visitors would question the monks about the monastery and then write a report for Thomas Cromwell.

Examiner's advice

The answer requires a point-by-point comparison of the sources and not simply a paragraph on each one. You should start by considering the main message of each source – do they agree or disagree? Why? This is where you can consider their provenance, as it is likely that this will help to explain their similarity or difference. Look for other points of comparison and again explain them by considering their provenance.

When you have made two or three points of comparison, you should be able to reach a judgement about which source is the most useful as evidence for the condition of the monasteries.

Do note that you are not being asked to bring in lots of your own knowledge to answer the question.

Valor Ecclesiasticus

A record of the wealth and income of the Church. Cromwell had sent out commissioners in 1535 to collect these details.

Norman Conquest

When William the Conquerer conquered England in 1066, most English landholders lost their land to Norman nobles.

prayers for the dead

It was believed that praying for the souls of the dead could reduce their time in purgatory.

purgatory

It was believed that in order to go straight to heaven, a soul had to be free from sin. Most were not, and so went to a halfway place: purgatory. They would stay there until they were ready to go to heaven; the length of time depended upon the sins they had committed.

chantries

Small chapels where prayers for the dead were said to reduce their time in purgatory.

A survey of all the income of the Church then followed, through the **Valor Ecclesiasticus**. The evidence from this and the visitation was presented to Parliament in 1536 and the Act closing the smaller monasteries was passed. This Act criticised the behaviour of the monks in the smaller monasteries, but it praised the larger ones: 'The various and great solemn monasteries of this realm; wherein thanks be to God, religion is well kept and observed.'

ACTIVITY

1   Why do you think the Act of 1536 praised the larger monasteries?

2   What might be the purpose of the statement?

3   What does this suggest about the reasons for the closure of the smaller monasteries? How far is this view supported by the reports of the visitations?

Only four years later all the larger houses had also been closed down. Much of this took place between 1537 and 1539; little force was needed and the Act only confirmed what had already taken place.

The Act dissolving the smaller monasteries suggests that it had not been Henry's intention in 1536 to dissolve all the monasteries. It may be that the reaction of northern England to this Act, through the rebellion known as the Pilgrimage of Grace (see Chapter 5, pages 126–130), convinced him that the monasteries would be centres of opposition to his changes. It is also possible that Cromwell saw in the monasteries the opportunity to make Henry financially independent of Parliament and use the land as a source of patronage to prevent further opposition. It appears that Henry was fearful of opposition to the second Act, as a further Act promising to use monasteries as cathedrals and for educational purposes was put through Parliament at the same time. Its timing supports the argument that its purpose was to disarm potential opponents; if that was the case, it certainly worked, as the Act passed with ease.

The dissolution resulted in the largest transfer of land since the **Norman Conquest** and provided Henry with a vast reservoir of patronage that could be used to reward loyal servants and supporters. The proceeds would also finance the extensive building of fortifications on the south coast in readiness for possible attack from Spain and France.

The dissolution meant that some people lost their local church and had to travel further to attend services. It also appeared to represent an attack on **prayers for the dead**, as monasteries were the very place where this practice was undertaken. It could therefore be argued that the dissolution represented a significant attack on traditional Catholic practices. However, it must be remembered that in 1547 the singing of masses for the souls of the dead was still allowed and that Henry himself left money in his will for this. The position of **purgatory** was less clear: no firm statement had been made and the failure to implement the Act dissolving **chantries** only added to the uncertainty.

ACTIVITY

Why were the larger houses closed down? What was the significance of this?

How significant were the Ten Articles and Act of Six Articles?

The Ten Articles were issued to further an alliance with the German Protestant princes, but the articles did not take a distinctly Protestant view. Most importantly, the articles declared that at the mass Christ's body and blood were present 'substantially', leaving the interpretation open to both Catholic and Lutheran views. They also claimed that **salvation** could be obtained by 'contrition and faith joined with charity'. Once again, this suggests that the Catholic belief in good works to achieve salvation was still important. Although it might be argued that the Act acknowledged only three of the seven sacraments – the Eucharist, Baptism and Penance – as necessary for salvation, it did not condemn the other four (see Chapter 1, page 12). It is also worth noting that these articles did not have the force of law as they were not passed by Parliament. Overall, it appears as if the Act avoided many of the controversial issues, or at least left them ambiguous for fear of upsetting either side.

If the Ten Articles were ambiguous, the Six Articles were a clear statement that England was still a Catholic country. The Six Articles upheld the key Catholic doctrine of transubstantiation and affirmed clerical celibacy, communion in one kind for the laity, the importance of masses for the dead and confession (see Chapter 1, page 12). This act was passed by Parliament and therefore it can be clearly argued that Catholic beliefs were being upheld by law. Those who denied any of these beliefs were liable to burning, hanging or life imprisonment.

It is clear that taken together, the Articles upheld Catholic beliefs until Henry died.

To what extent did the royal injunctions of 1536 and 1538 make England more Protestant?

If the sets of articles did little to establish Protestantism, it can be argued that the two sets of **injunctions** did destroy elements of traditional Catholic ceremonial.

The 1536 injunctions placed considerable emphasis on religious education for the young. Although this was not an attack on Catholicism, priests were also to encourage support for the Royal Supremacy and the Ten Articles. More importantly, the injunctions reduced the number of Holy Days and required the clergy to provide Bibles in English and Latin for people to read. This was significant as instead of only priests being able to read and interpret the Bible, ordinary people now had the opportunity to read and interpret it for themselves. This would undermine the clergy's claim to be the sole interpreters of scripture.

The 1538 injunctions continued the move towards Protestantism. However, it should be remembered that they were issued when Henry was pursuing an alliance with the German Lutheran princes. There were attacks on images that were the object of pilgrimages, and sermons against the worshipping of images and relics were to be preached (see Chapter 1, pages 13–14).

Taken together, the injunctions suggest that there was a clear move away from Catholic ritual and ceremonial and the establishment of Protestant beliefs. However, the Ten and Six Articles contradict this and show that England was still Catholic in doctrine.

salvation

Avoidance of hell and entry to heaven.

injunctions

A series of orders and instructions issued by Thomas Cromwell to priests about what should be taught and the decoration in churches. They were used to promote the new religion.

How important was the Bishop's Book of 1537?

At the same time as finding the four lost sacraments, Henry also insisted that the book should give due weight to the role of good works, not just faith, in achieving salvation (see Chapter 1, pages 12–13).

Source

C **Read the following extract from the Bishop's Book. This book was officially called '*The Institution of a Christian Man*'. It was the subject of much debate between conservative and reformist bishops. However, most importantly it lacked royal approval, as the King claimed he lacked the time to look at it; when he finally did, he sent Cranmer 250 changes.**

*Although the sacraments of matrimony, of confirmation, of holy orders, and of **extreme unction**, have been of long time past received and approved by the common consent of the Catholic church, to have the name and dignity of sacraments, as indeed they be well worthy to have, yet there is a difference in dignity and necessity between them and the other three sacraments of baptism, of penance, and of the altar.*

extreme unction

The anointing of a dying person with holy oil, similar to the anointing of a priest at ordination.

ACTIVITY

Compare the attitude of the Bishop's Book (Source C) to the Seven Sacraments with those outlined in the Ten Articles (page 65).

ACTIVITY

Consider how far the reforms of 1536 to 1538 had moved England in a Protestant direction. What is your view? What is your evidence to support this view?

Think about the sources you have read. How useful are they in explaining what was happening in the localities? What was the purpose of the acts and injunctions? Do they provide any evidence that the reforms were being implemented? Source D might help you reach a conclusion.

diocese

The area of administration under the control of a bishop.

Source

D *The Injunctions of 1536 and 1538 seemed royal waves in the offensive heretical tide. There were reports of disobedience to the first Injunctions from the **dioceses** of Exeter, Salisbury and Worcester in the south-west, and Chichester, Canterbury and Norwich in the south-east; a parson in Suffolk refused to preach against the pope and waved the Ten Articles before his congregation warning, 'Beware, my friends, of the English books!' There was even more widespread hostility to the Second Injunctions; they were dismissed by a London rector as 'a thing to make fools afraid'. Parishes were slow to buy the required Bibles; very few outside London and the cathedral cities had done so within two years.*

Christopher Haigh (1993) *English Reformations*. Oxford University Press.

How far did England become a Protestant country in the 1540s?

Many historians have seen the period as one of religious uncertainty, but a few common themes emerge.

Source

E In 1546 Anne Askew, a Lincolnshire woman, was put on trial for denying the Real Presence. Before being burnt, she was tortured to try to get her to implicate ladies of the Queen's Privy Chamber as heretics. It was hoped that she might implicate Queen Catherine Parr. The following is an extract from her Examinations.

They said to me there, that I was a heretic, and condemned by the law, if I would stand in my opinion. I answered that I was no heretic, neither yet deserved I any death by the law of God: but as concerning the faith which I uttered and wrote to the Council, I would not, I said, deny it, because I knew it true. Then would they needs know if I would deny the sacrament to be Christ's body and blood. I said, Yes, for the same Son of God that was born of the Virgin Mary, is now glorious in heaven, and will come again from there.

ACTIVITY

1   What crime was Askew accused of?

2   What does this tell us about moves towards Protestantism?

Askew was found guilty of denying the **Real Presence** and was burnt alive, having previously been tortured to try to get her to implicate ladies of the Queen's Chamber and possibly Queen Catherine Parr herself as heretics. This attack on Askew at virtually the end of Henry's reign supports the view that the King maintained his belief in the Real Presence throughout his reign; it can be compared with the treatment given to John Lambert in 1538 (see Source F below).

Real Presence

The belief that in the mass the body and blood of Christ were present in the bread and wine.

Source

F Lambert had also been accused of denying the Real Presence in the Eucharist. Henry himself attended the trial, dressed all in white as a clear sign of his commitment against heresy. The following account of the trial is taken from **Foxe's** *Book of Martyrs* and therefore needs to be read with caution.

Lambert was brought in to open court and forced to defend his cause. The King commanded Cranmer to refute Lambert's assertion that the body of Christ was not present in the sacrament of the altar. ... When they had contended, Lambert answered so well that the King seemed to be greatly moved, the Archbishop entangled and the audience amazed. Then the Bishop of Winchester, fearing that the argument would be lost, interrupted the Archbishop. Through the evil counsel of this one Bishop of Winchester, Satan did here perform the condemnation of Lambert.

ACTIVITY

1   What evidence is there in Source F that Foxe was sympathetic to Lambert?

2   How similar were the charges brought against Askew and Lambert?

3   What does this tell us about Henry's attitude towards any change in the Catholic doctrine of the Mass? What does this suggest about moves towards Protestantism in the period from 1538 to 1546?

Foxe's Book of Martyrs

John Foxe was a Protestant who, on Mary Tudor's accession to the throne, fled to the Protestant city of Strasbourg. He returned to England on the accession of Elizabeth and wrote his *Book of Martyrs*, which gave a detailed account of the sufferings and burnings of Protestants in England. It became a bestseller.

Figure 3.1   John Foxe.

Lambert was found guilty and was burnt alive on 22 November 1538. Henry followed this up by issuing a proclamation asserting the Real Presence and the observance of church ceremonies. If these actions were clear signs of the limits of Henry's willingness to move towards Protestant beliefs, they were reinforced by the removal of his reforming minister, Thomas Cromwell, in 1540 (see Chapter 2, pages 39–40).

ACTIVITY

Read Source G.

1   Which key Catholic beliefs did the King's Book uphold?

2   How far did the King's Book support the view expressed at the trials of Lambert and Askew?

3   What does this tell us about continuity in Henry's religious beliefs?

At the same time, the King's Book upheld confession, allowed the use of images (provided they were used without superstition) and clearly rejected the Protestant view of justification by faith.

Perhaps the clearest indication of moves towards Protestantism in the 1530s had been the appearance of the Great Bible in 1539. Although widespread illiteracy would in practice prevent many from reading the Bible, potentially it gave everyone access to the word of God and the opportunity to interpret the scriptures for themselves. In 1543 the Act for the Advancement of True Religion did much to alter the situation. It condemned 'crafty, false and untrue' translations of the Bible and severely limited who could read it. Noblemen and gentlemen might read it to their families at home, while merchants might read it to themselves, but common people were not to read it at all. Once again, any limited moves towards Protestantism had been reversed.

Source

(G) **If the Bishop's Book was seen as having some conservative elements, a reading of the King's Book, produced in 1543, only adds to the view that moves towards Protestantism were very limited. Read the following extracts from the King's Book.**

For he that receives the sacrament worthily under the one kind, as under the form of bread only, receives the whole body and blood of Christ, and as many and great benefits of Christ that he who receives it in both kinds. Therefore if any man should teach that the lay people are tricked and cause them to think that the whole body and blood of Christ were not present just in the bread, as well as in both kinds, this doctrine ought to be utterly denied.

Wherefore as we continue and persevere in good works, so more and more we go forward and proceed in our justification, and in increasing the same. And to ascribe this dignity unto good works, it is no derogation to the grace of God; forasmuch it is to be confessed that all good works come of the grace of God. And our merits be but the gifts of God.

Source

(H) **Read the following extract from this modern historian's work on the English Reformations:**

The limitation of Bible-reading was a tragedy for Protestant ministers; it was a triumph for the conservative bishops and their supporters. They had now undone almost all that Cromwell had achieved between 1536 and 1538. They had taken advantage of Henry VIII's own conservatism, his fear of popular protest, and his wish for an imperial alliance against France. They had imposed transubstantiation and confession in the Six Articles; they had killed Cromwell and frightened Cranmer into compliance. They had promoted heresy hunts, which were not severe enough to destroy heresy but were regular enough to contain its expansion, and they had convinced the king that orthodoxy must be maintained by force. In 1543, they had got the King's Book, which had rejected justification by faith and defended the traditional sacraments, and they had gained a prohibition of Bible-reading by the majority of the people. By the spring of 1543 the Protestant elements of the first Reformation had been reversed; only the break with Rome and the suppression of the monasteries survived.

Christopher Haigh (1993) *English Reformations*. Oxford University Press.

Stretch and challenge

Read Source H, then answer the following questions.

1   What is Haigh's view about the progress of the Reformation by 1543?

2   What evidence does he put forward to support his view?

3   Using evidence from this chapter, how far do you agree with his view?

Source

I Despite the lack of success for the supporters of Protestantism, it was still necessary for Henry VIII to make a speech to Parliament in 1545, appealing for religious peace in the country:

I see and hear daily that you clergymen preach against each other, teach contrary to each other, condemn each other without charity or discretion. Some are still too stiff in their old views; others are too busy and curious in their new opinions. Thus all men are religiously divided, and few or none preach the word of God as they should, truly and sincerely. The people look for light from you preachers, and instead you bring them into darkness. Change your ways, I urge you, or I will suppress these divisions through my authority as Supreme Head of the Church.

ACTIVITY

1   What does Source I tell us about the religious situation in England in 1546?

2   Why do you think that the situation outlined by Henry has developed?

3   What does Henry see to be his role in religious matters?

4   Why do you think Henry would be so concerned?

5   Compare the views put forward in Source I with that expressed by Haigh in Source H.

If there was to be any joy for the Protestants, it came in the last year of Henry's reign. Wars against France and Scotland had brought two reformers to prominence: Edward Seymour and John Dudley (see Chapter 2, pages 51–54). These men, with the help of William Paget and Anthony Denny (see Chapter 2, page 30), were able to remove the conservative or Catholic faction from the King's Council. This allowed the reformers to control Henry's will and seize control when he died, as during Henry's reign, their motives were much more linked to gaining political power than to advancing the cause of Protestantism.

What was the religious situation in England on the death of Henry VIII?

When Henry died, despite the break with Rome and the number of changes, England was still largely following traditional Catholic beliefs, although there were a few Protestant practices.

Catholic practices	Protestant practices
The Catholic form of the **Eucharist** was still followed and transubstantiation was upheld	There was more importance attached to the sermon
Only the clergy could take communion in both kinds	The **Lord's Prayer, Creed** and **Ten Commandments** had to be taught in English
The seven sacraments had been affirmed after 1539	It was forbidden to make pilgrimages
The laity still had to go to confession	There were no monasteries
The clergy were not allowed to marry and those who had done so had to send their wives away	
The need for good works in order to achieve salvation had been reinstated	
The singing of masses for the souls of the dead was still acceptable	
Paintings and statues were allowed in churches, although people were not allowed to worship them	
The services were still in Latin	Cranmer's prayers and the responses of the litany were in English
No specific statement had been made on purgatory.	

Table 3.1   Religious practices in England at the death of Henry VIII.

> **Lord's Prayer, Creed, Ten Commandments**
>
> These set out the basic beliefs and prayers of the Church. If these were in English, everyone would be able to understand them.

Who did more to make England a Protestant nation, Somerset or Northumberland?

There has been a great deal of debate about the progress of the Reformation under Edward VI, particularly about the contributions of the two Protectors, Somerset and Northumberland (see Chapter 2, pages 51–54). Many have argued that progress under Somerset was limited, but that it speeded up under the more radical Northumberland. However, it must be remembered that Somerset had first to remove Catholic practices before any Protestant ones could be introduced. It would then be much easier for Northumberland to embark on a more radical programme. The other area of debate concerns the success in implementing the changes at grass roots. Edward ruled for only six years, and historians have questioned how far it was possible to turn the nation Protestant in such a short space of time, particularly as there was such limited support for Protestantism on Edward's accession.

This section will be split into two parts; the first will consider the extent of the changes and their results, the second will consider their impact on the ordinary people of England.

Source

J The progress of the Reformation under Somerset and Northumberland was quite slow. Read the following passage by a modern historian.

*In 1548 the **Council** ordered the removal of all images from churches. Though the first Prayer Book (1549) had a very moderate and conservative appearance, the steady progress of reform continued. In November 1550 a campaign was launched to remove all stone altars and replace them with wooden communion tables. This was a clear recognition that the Eucharist was no longer seen as a sacrifice, as suggested by the altar, but simply an act of remembrance. With the advent of the second Prayer Book (1552), the worship of the English could be described as fully reformed. However, the Forty-Two Articles, containing the doctrine of the Church, were not issued until June 1553, less than a month before Edward's death.*

David Loades (1992) *Mid Tudor Crisis, 1545–1565*. Palgrave Macmillan.

Council

The ministers and advisors who were now running the country as Edward VI was too young to rule. However, Somerset largely ignored them and ruled on his own.

ACTIVITY

1   Somerset fell from power in October 1549; what does Source J suggest about the progress of Protestantism under Somerset and Northumberland?

2   How far does Source J support the view that the English Church was fully reformed by the death of Edward?

3   As the Forty-Two Articles were not issued until June 1553, what impact are they likely to have had by the time Edward died?

Now read Source K, a passage from Haigh's *English Reformations*.

Source

K A modern historian describes the changes brought about by Edward's reforms.

*King Edward's Church had come a long way since 1547. The mass was replaced by a reformed communion, the King's Book by the Forty Two Articles; and in 1553 there was a Protestant Short **Catechism** and a book of private prayers. The political interests of Somerset and Northumberland, the influence of Cranmer and Ridley, the pressures of Hooper and Knox, and the demands of grass-roots Protestantism carried Edward's second reformation very much further than Henry VIII's first.*

Christopher Haigh (1993) *English Reformations*. Oxford University Press.

catechism

A religious book on key aspects of belief, set out in a question-and-answer form.

Stretch and challenge

How similar are Haigh's and Loades' views about the implementation of Protestantism?

The extent of the religious changes

Table 3.2 lists the major religious changes in the period from 1547 to the death of Edward in 1553. You should be able to explain briefly the importance of each change.

Date	Change	What the changes meant	Effect
July 1547	Book of **Homilies**	A series of Protestant sermons for those priests who were unable to preach effectively. It also allowed the government to put across reformist religious views	Prevented Catholic preaching
July 1547	Royal Injunctions	These ordered the clergy to preach in English and have an English Bible in the church	Removed superstitious images
Nov/Dec 1547	Dissolution of the Chantries	An attack on the Catholic doctrine of purgatory, which also brought the government much-needed wealth	Condemned Catholic belief in prayers for the dead
Nov/Dec 1547	Act of Six Articles repealed	The Act of Six Articles had restored much Catholic doctrine in 1539; this removed it	Removed key Catholic doctrines
Jan–March 1548	Proclamations to lessen Protestant unrest	There was a great deal of radical Protestant preaching and the government needed to reassert its control	Lack of doctrine had meant disorder; government now tried to control it
Feb 1548	Images to be removed	A further attack on Catholic practices; their removal with little evidence of opposition might suggest support for the move	Attacked Catholic practice
April 1548	Only authorised clergy to preach	Once again the government was concerned about the radical nature of some of the preaching	Attempted to stop radical preaching and maintain order
Dec 1548	First Prayer Book	A compromise designed to appeal to moderate Catholics and Protestants (see page 75)	Still had Catholic elements
Jan 1549	First Act of Uniformity	This made the Prayer Book the official service	Made the Prayer Book the official liturgy

Homilies

Government-produced sermons so that uneducated priests had ready-made sermons available. They were used to put across key beliefs, such as obedience.

Ordinal

A book outlining the service for the ordination of priests.

Dec 1549	Proclamation orders destruction of remaining images	Their issuing suggests that the order in February 1548 to remove all images had not been successful and that the appeal of traditional Catholic practices was still strong	Further attack on Catholic practices
Jan 1550	New **Ordinal**	This set out the service for the ordination of new clergy; it was unpopular with more radical Protestants as it required the clergy to wear white surplices and swear an oath to saints	Still had Catholic element as included oath to saints
Nov 1550	Stone altars removed and replaced with wooden tables	A clear sign of the changing nature of the Eucharist service: a stone altar had suggested sacrifice, a wooden table suggested a simple meal and the idea that the service was simply remembrance	Attempted to remove idea of sacrifice from Eucharist
Jan 1552	Second Book of Common Prayer	This was fully Protestant, following many Calvinist beliefs (see page 75)	Highly Protestant
April 1552	Second Act of Uniformity	The second Prayer Book was the official service and it was an offence not to attend church	Enforced Second Prayer Book
Nov 1552	Forty-Two Articles	These set out the beliefs of the Edwardian Church and were highly Protestant, including the belief in justification by faith and predestination. With Edward's death they never became law, but they would be the basis of Elizabeth's settlement and 39 Articles	Strongly Protestant

Table 3.2 The major religious changes in the period from 1547 to the death of Edward in 1553.

As Table 3.2 shows, many of the early changes simply saw the destruction of remaining Catholic practices; this was followed by a period when the Church was left without a clear doctrine, before there was a gradual move in a Protestant direction, which was only completed with the publication of the Second Prayer Book in the last few months of Edward's reign. The slow and gradual nature of these changes would also have an impact on their adoption at grass roots.

Sources

(L) **The slow move towards Protestantism is made clear by comparing the following extracts from the Edwardian Prayer Books. This extract is from the 1549 Book of Common Prayer.**

Grant us therefore gracious Lord so to eat the flesh of your dear Son Jesus Christ, and to drink his blood, that we may continually dwell in him, and he in us. Amen.

And the minister, delivering the Sacrament of the body of Christ shall say:

The body of our Lord Jesus Christ which is given for you, preserve your body and soul unto everlasting life.

And the minister delivering the Sacrament of the blood, and giving it to everyone to drink, shall say:

The blood of our Lord Jesus Christ which was shed for you, preserve your body and soul unto everlasting life.

(M) **This extract is from the Second Book of Common Prayer, issued in 1552.**

Hear us O merciful Father we beg you; and grant that we, receiving these your gifts of bread and wine, according to Christ's example, in remembrance of his death, may share in his most blessed body and blood.

And when the minister delivers the bread, he shall say:

Take and eat this, in remembrance that Christ died for you, and feed on him in your heart by faith, with thanksgiving.

And when the minister delivers the cup, he shall say:

Drink this in remembrance that Christ's blood was shed for you, and be thankful.

ACTIVITY

Before tackling these questions it would be worthwhile revisiting the section in Chapter 1, pages 12–14, which outlines the religious beliefs of Catholics and Protestants.

1   How similar are the versions of the service presented in Sources L and M?

In order to answer this question, think carefully about the following:

■ What is the main message being put forward in each extract? What evidence from the passages do you have to support this?

■ What do the passages tell you about the congregation receiving both bread and wine?

■ In what ways does Source L put forward views that might appeal to conservative or Catholic elements in society? In what ways are these still present in Source M?

■ In what ways does Source L put forward views that might appeal to Protestant elements in society? In what ways are these still present in Source M?

2   What is your overall view about the similarity of the two passages? How far do they agree?

The progression between the two prayer books is perhaps the clearest example of the Church moving in a more Protestant direction under Northumberland. Both governments faced serious problems in trying to introduce religious changes. Somerset's government, despite only moderate changes to the Prayer Book in 1549, faced the Western Rebellion (see Chapter 5), which was largely a response to the religious changes he had introduced. Meanwhile, Northumberland's government faced other difficulties in trying to take the country in a more Protestant direction.

Source

N This extract from a letter by **Martin Bucer** to **John Calvin** in June 1550 outlines some of the issues and summarises some of the religious problems that Northumberland inherited from Somerset.

The Bishops have not yet agreed on Christian doctrine, let alone the rules of the Church, and very few parishes have qualified clergymen. Sometimes the clergy read the service rapidly, so that the ordinary people have no more understanding of it than if it were still in Latin rather than English. When these problems are presented to the Bishops, they say they cannot correct them without an Act of Parliament. Though Parliament meets every year, the number of secular matters stops Church affairs being discussed. When you next write to the Duke of Somerset, you must urge him to reform the Church.

BIOGRAPHIES

Martin Bucer

A Swiss Protestant reformer who came to England during the reign of Edward VI.

John Calvin

(1509–64) A French-born Protestant reformer who established the Calvinist Church in Geneva, Switzerland. He was quite radical in his views, believing that the Church did not need bishops and that God had already chosen those who would go to heaven – this was known as predestination. He also believed in justification by faith and wanted to establish a very simple Church.

Anabaptists

Protestant extremists, most notable for their activities in the north German town of Munster, where they had introduced communism and polygamy. They burned books, apart from the Bible, and were willing to put unbelievers to death.

ACTIVITY

1   Martin Bucer was a leading Protestant reformer; why might he be disappointed by the progress of the Reformation?

2   How might this affect the reliability of his comments?

Source

O Now read the following from Bishop Hooper, ordering the clergy in Gloucester diocese to teach the official Protestant faith and to condemn both Catholic and more radical Protestant ideas.

*You must condemn the doctrines of the **Anabaptists**, who deny the christening of infants, who believe that goods should be held in common, and who state that lay rulers have no power in the Church of God.*

You must teach that the salvation of people results from faith in Jesus Christ, not by the merit of good works.

You must condemn the idea of prayers for the dead and worshipping of saints and images.

You must teach that at communion there is no changing of the bread and wine into the body and blood of Christ.

ACTIVITY

In Source O, what problems does Hooper identify in imposing Protestantism in the diocese of Gloucester?

What are the limitations of Source O in explaining the problems in imposing Protestantism in England in the reign of Edward VI?

Compare Sources N and O as evidence for the problems in imposing Protestantism in England in the reign of Edward VI.

Examiner's advice

- In order to tackle this question, identify the main problem in imposing Protestantism that is outlined in each passage. Are they similar or different?

- What other problems does each passage identify? What similarities and differences are there? Ensure that you can support each with a short quotation from the passage.

- Now think about the provenance of each passage. Why might the passages adopt their particular point of view? Think about author and purpose. How will these impact on their reliability?

- You now need to reach a judgement about which source offers the best explanation for the problems in imposing Protestantism, based on the previous questions. If you follow this approach, you should be able to access the higher levels in the mark grid.

Source

(P) The difficulties in imposing a more Protestant form of worship were also made clear in the Second Act of Uniformity of 1552. The Act stated that:

*In spite of the introduction of the **First Book of Common Prayer** by Parliament, a great number of people in this realm wilfully and damnably refuse to come to their parish churches on Sundays and holy days. In future those who are absent shall be punished by the Church courts. The First Common Prayer Book has produced doubts about the form of worship, so the King has ordered a Second Book of Common Prayer to replace it. Anyone who uses another form of worship shall be imprisoned for six months.*

ACTIVITY

Read Source P.

1   What problem does the Act identify?

2   What pressures will be placed on the people to ensure acceptance of the Second Prayer Book?

3   What is the significance of the date of the Act?

4   Compare Source P with Hooper's instructions to his diocese as evidence of the problems in imposing Protestantism (Source O).

First Book of Common Prayer

This was written by Cranmer and was to be used from June 1549. It was in English and adopted a moderate view of the Eucharist service. There is greater reference to the contents on page 75.

Northumberland's reforms were more radical in their nature and because he faced no religiously motivated rebellions it could be argued that he was more successful in imposing Protestantism than Somerset. However, Sources N, O and P suggest that this was far from the case and that even at the end of the period there were still difficulties in bringing about religious change. This view can be contrasted with the view put forward by Edward's former tutor, Sir John Cheke, a committed Protestant, in a letter to a reformer in one of the Protestant cities of Switzerland.

Source

(Q) **Read this extract from a letter by Sir John Cheke to a Protestant reformer in Switzerland. It was written in 1553, before Edward died.**

The King has accomplished more in his youth than many have done in their adult life. He has repealed the Act of the Six Articles. He has removed images from churches. He has overthrown image worship. He has abolished the mass, and destroyed almost every kind of superstition. He has published good and pious homilies to lessen the ignorance of uneducated ministers. Each of these achievements would be considered a great action in other men, but as nothing to him, given the very great amount he has accomplished.

ACTIVITY

Compare Source Q with Source N as evidence for the success in imposing Protestantism during the reign of Edward VI.

The sources put forward different views about the success of the Edwardian Reformation, yet both are written by Protestants. You have already considered the reliability of Bucer's comments, but you now need to think about the reliability of Cheke. Why might he stress the success of the reforms and the importance of the King? How might this affect the reliability of the source?

In comparing the sources' provenance it would be worthwhile thinking about their purpose. Why were they written? More important in explaining the different views might be their dates. When were they written? How might this affect their point of view?

What was the impact of the changes on the people of England?

If England was still largely Catholic in belief on the death of Henry VIII, it is not surprising that the progress of the Reformation under Edward was slow. After centuries of Catholicism, conversion would not happen overnight and it is understandable that there was opposition at a local level, as was seen in the Western Rebellion of 1549, (see Chapter 5).

Source

(R) **The slow progress of the Reformation is illustrated by the following comment from Sir William Paget (see Chapter 2, pages 30 and 31), writing to Somerset in the summer of 1549.**

Look well whether you have law or religion at home, and I fear you shall find neither. The use of the old religion is forbidden by a law, and the use of the new is not yet printed in the stomachs of the eleven of twelve parts of the realm.

Source R was written over two years into Edward's reign and suggests that the progress of the Reformation was slow. This is further emphasised by the reaction in the Western Rebellion to the very moderate changes made to the Prayer Book.

It is apparent from Acts of Parliament under Northumberland's administration that the progress of the Reformation had been slow. This is made clearer in Source S, where the government has to take action for a third time against images.

Source

(S) **In 1550, Parliament condemns Catholic service books and completes the campaign, started in 1548, against images in churches.**

The King has issued through Parliament a uniform, quiet and godly order of service called the Book of Common Prayer, which contains nothing but the pure word of God. However, alongside it are still practised corrupt, untrue and superstitious ceremonies, which allow some to attack the order and meaning of the Prayer Book and encourage great diversity of opinion. Therefore it is ordered that all books used for the old mass be abolished, and any images of stone, timber or marble be defaced and destroyed.

An Act for the abolition and putting away of images and various books, 1550.

ACTIVITY

1   According to Source S, what has been the impact of the Edwardian Reformation on the parishes?

2   How reliable is Source S in explaining the progress of the Edwardian Reformation? In order to answer this, you need to think carefully about the date and the purpose of the source.

Now read Source T.

1   In what ways does Hutton's account offer a different view of the progress of the Reformation?

2   What evidence does he put forward to support his view?

churchwarden's accounts

Churchwardens were responsible for the finances of a church. Their accounts can often be used to show how far they followed the government's instructions.

Source

(T) **Historians have put forward different views about the impact of the Reformation at the local level. Read the following extract from Ronald Hutton's 'The local impact of the Tudor Reformation'.**

*The impact [of Protector Somerset's regime] was devastating: the great majority of the decorations and rites employed in and around English churches in early 1547 had gone by late 1549. As far as **churchwardens' accounts** tell the story, all that the succeeding radical administration of Northumberland had to do was to 'mop up' by revising the Prayer Book, replacing the altars with communion tables and confiscating the obsolete church goods. The new service was introduced in every parish in the sample study within the prescribed period in 1552–53, and other reforms were just as thoroughly carried out, although over a longer period.*

Ronald Hutton (1987) 'The local impact of the Tudor Reformation', in C. Haigh, *The English Reformation Revised*, CUP.

The view of Hutton is challenged by the Second Act of Uniformity in 1552, which condemned people's absence from church and imposed the Second Book of Common Prayer.

Source

 Read this extract from the Second Act of Uniformity, 1552.

In spite of the introduction of the First Common Prayer Book by Parliament, a great number of people in this realm wilfully and damnably refuse to come to their parish churches on Sundays and holy days. In future those who are absent shall be punished by Church courts. The First Common Prayer Book has produced doubts about the form of worship, so the King has ordered a Second Book of Common Prayer to replace it. Anyone who uses another form of worship shall be imprisoned for six months.

ACTIVITY

Compare Sources S and U as evidence for the ways in which the Edwardian Reformation was implemented.

It is difficult to chart the progress and success of the Edwardian Reformation. Sources S and U suggest that the government had not won over the hearts of the people to Protestantism, whereas Source T suggests otherwise. By the end of Edward's reign, parliamentary statutes suggest that a full-scale Protestant Reformation had been ordered, but the acceptance of these measures varied from parish to parish.

Source

 Now read the following passage from Eamon Duffy's *The Stripping of the Altars*:

There were parishes where the reform was embraced with ardour, at least by those with most influence, and where a new solidarity began to emerge on the basis of the new faith.

Even in communities where this was not so, the passage of time and the relentless push of the Council policy had its effect. The men and women of Tudor England were, by and large, pragmatists. Grumbling, they sold off as much of their Catholic past as they could not hide or keep, and called in the carpenters to set boards on trestles and fix the forms round the communion tables. Used to obedience, many of them accepted the changes, however unwelcome, as unavoidable. Four years of exposure to the matchless and memorable dignity of Cranmer's English services could not be without effect.

Eamon Duffy (2005) *The Stripping of the Altars*. Yale.

ACTIVITY

1   What is Duffy's view of the success of the Edwardian Reformation?

2   How far does he agree with Hutton's view in Source T?

> ### Source
>
> **Finally, read the following extract from David Loades' *Mid Tudor Crisis, 1545–1565*:**
>
> *The Protestantism of Edward VI's reign was not a natural growth, it was highly artificial and imposed by authority; nevertheless it was successfully imposed. Although vestments, images and liturgical books were often taken away and hidden, conformity was effectively enforced upon the parish churches. Not only were the ecclesiastical authorities surprisingly energetic in this respect, they were well backed up by the secular authorities.*
>
> David Loades (1992) *Mid Tudor Crisis, 1545–1565*. Palgrave Macmillan.

> ### Stretch and challenge
>
> Having read various extracts from historians, it is time to frame your own view about the success of the Edwardian Reformation at the parish level. In order to do this, consider the questions below. (Note that you would not get a question like this in the exam, but it is useful to organise your thoughts about the different views.)
>
> 1 Did most people accept the religious changes of Edward's reign?
>
> 2 How much evidence is there that this was because they welcomed the changes or because the authorities were able to enforce the new practices on them?
>
> 3 How much evidence is there of opposition to the changes? Why do you think this was the case?
>
> 4 Mary Tudor was able to restore England to the Catholic faith with relative ease. What does this tell you about the overall success of the Edwardian Reformation?

How successful was Mary in restoring Catholicism?

There has been much debate among historians about the success of Mary's religious policies. It used to be the accepted view that her attempts to restore Catholicism were doomed to failure. Supporters of this view argued that her policies met with considerable opposition in Parliament, that the burnings of Protestants turned many away from Catholicism and that her failure to produce an heir only confirmed her lack of success. More recent work has shown that what little opposition there was in Parliament was not on religious grounds, that the burnings had little impact and that it was the lack of an heir that ultimately ensured her failure. This view has been reinforced by a study of Elizabeth's early years, which has shown the difficulties she faced in introducing Protestantism.

It would have come as little surprise to most English people that Mary wanted to restore Catholicism. She had resisted the Royal Supremacy for 20 years and her success against Lady Jane Grey (see Chapter 5) served only to reinforce her view that it was not only her duty, but also her destiny, to restore England to the Catholic faith.

Source

X At the start of her reign, Mary proceeded with great caution, as the following proclamation from August 1553 makes clear.

Her Majesty will observe the Catholic religion she has professed all her life, and desires that all her subjects would quietly follow suit. However she will not compel any to this until further decisions are made. She commands her subjects to live together in Christian charity, avoiding the new and devilish terms of papist and heretic, and trying to live peaceful Christian lives. Any man who stirs up the people to disorder will be severely punished. Printers have published books and ballads written in English which discuss controversial religious teaching. Let nobody do so in future without the Queen's express permission.

ACTIVITY

Read Source X.

1 What is the purpose of the proclamation?

2 Why would Mary proceed with caution at this stage in her reign?

sung mass

A service similar to the usual mass, but the main prayers were sung in Latin rather than spoken.

Although Mary began her reign in a cautious manner, many people welcomed her succession. In Melton Mowbray, Leicestershire, church bells were rung in celebration and Parliament opened with a **sung mass**, which was still officially illegal. The large numbers who turned out to watch her coronation were in stark contrast to those who attended Lady Jane Grey's. All of this suggests that Mary's goal of restoring England to Catholicism had every chance of success as she enjoyed widespread support.

How successful was Mary in winning parliamentary approval for her religious policies?

The arrest of leading Protestant bishops had removed potential opponents from the House of Lords, yet there was a distinct lack of religious opposition when Parliament met in October 1553. Parliament did refuse to repeal the Act of Supremacy, but it passed an Act of Repeal that undid all of the Edwardian Reformation, taking the Church back to where it had been in 1547. By the end of the year Mary had also given up her title of Supreme Head of the Church.

Source

Y The Imperial Ambassador recalls Pole's speech to Parliament on his return to England, and gives a clear indication of feelings about a restoration to papal authority.

Yesterday, Parliament came to the unanimous decision that all laws and statutes contrary to the Pope's authority should be repealed, the Church's authority be once more acknowledged, and the Cardinal admitted as Legate to carry out his mission. Although about 500 persons were gathered together, there was only one opposing voice, belonging to a man who enjoys no support, and there was no hint of making conditions about the Church property, but only an expression of confidence that the King and Queen would not allow the question to disrupt the reunion of England and Rome.

ACTIVITY

1 What is the Imperial Ambassador's view about the restoration of papal authority?

2 How reliable is the Imperial Ambassador's view?

The following year, Parliament met in November and passed the Second Act of Repeal. This Act returned England to papal authority and repealed all religious legislation passed after 1529. The issue of former **Church property** was a serious one for many Members of Parliament who had bought up the lands of former monasteries. This is made clear in Source Z.

The issue was still causing concern three months later, as is shown in Source Z.

Source

(Z) Concerns about ownership of former monastic lands are made clear in a letter from the Imperial Ambassador to Charles V in August 1554:

We decided that we should write to your Majesty that Cardinal Pole had better be persuaded to be patient for a little longer until we see how matters are going to turn out here. Above all, before coming to England, he must clear up this business of the position of the holders of Church property. The present possessors must be reassured that they will not have to hand back these lands, otherwise we shall never achieve the desired result. Unless he takes this advice he will run great risks himself and make the whole religious question more difficult.

ACTIVITY

Read Sources Y and Z.

How far does Source Z support Source Y about the difficulties in restoring former Church lands?

In order to ensure the passage of the Second Act of Repeal in 1554, Mary had to finally reach a compromise with the landowners. The Act protected the property rights of all those who had bought Church land since 1536, and it would prevent Mary from bringing about a full-scale restoration of monasticism.

Parliament also discussed the reintroduction of the heresy laws. At first this was rejected, not for religious reasons but because of a factional dispute between Gardiner and Paget, and because MPs wanted guarantees that former monastic lands would not be restored to the Church.

Church property

Many members of the ruling class had bought former Church lands following the dissolution of the monasteries. With England's return to Catholicism, the owners wanted reassurance that they would be allowed to keep the lands.

Figure 3.2   Simon Renard, Charles V's ambassador to England during the reign of Mary.

Source

AA The Imperial Ambassador's comments were astute, as his response to a sermon preached by the Dean of St Paul's in November 1554 shows in this extract from a letter to Charles V.

Last Sunday the Dean of St Paul's cathedral preached a sermon about the return of lands to the Church. It was disliked since he argued that the lay owners of former Church lands should now return them, even though they had obtained permission to own them. There was a general opinion that Cardinal Pole [see Chapter 2, page 55] had put the Dean up to this, but as the Dean has been sent for and reprimanded by the Council, it seems that he must have acted without the knowledge of the Council or of the Cardinal.

Therefore, by the end of 1554 England had been lifted from the sentence of excommunication and the Second Act of Repeal had restored England to the position of 1529. In order to achieve this, Mary had to reach a compromise with the landed elites and guarantee the property rights of those who had bought Church lands since 1536. Once again, opposition had been on economic rather than religious grounds. It would limit the restoration of Catholicism as Mary would have to forego her plans for a full-scale restoration of monasticism and be content with restoring just those lands still held by the Crown. This was achieved in 1556 with the re-foundation of the **Benedictine House** at Westminster and in 1557 with the re-founding of other smaller religious houses.

Benedictine House

A monastic house that followed the rule of St Benedict, an Italian monk of the fifth and sixth centuries. He drew up a set of rules for monastic life, which was to be the basis of the rules of all monastic orders in the Western Church.

Figure 3.3 The monasteries were wealthy and owned extensive lands.

What was the significance of Mary's policy of persecution?

Many accounts of the persecution of Protestants have put forward the view that it was ultimately the fires of **Smithfield** that turned England Protestant. They have argued that those who went to watch the burnings were so impressed by the commitment and steadfastness of those being persecuted that they were converted. Persecution started in 1555, following the restoration of the heresy laws, and continued until just days before Mary's death in 1558, with nearly 300 in total going to the stake.

Smithfield

A marketplace in London where many Protestants were burnt at the stake.

Figure 3.4   A public burning at Smithfield, London.

Source

BB **This view is upheld by the Imperial Ambassador, writing to Philip of Spain soon after the burnings began in February 1550:**

The people of London are murmuring about the cruel enforcement of the recent Act of Parliament against heresy which has now begun, as shown publicly when a certain Rogers was burnt yesterday. Some of the onlookers wept. Others prayed to God to give them strength, persistence, and patience to bear the pain and not to convert back to Catholicism. Others gathered the ashes and bones and wrapped them up in paper to preserve them. Yet others threatened the bishops. The haste with which the bishops have proceeded in this matter may well cause a revolt. If the people got the upper hand, not only would the cause of religion be again menaced, but the persons of your Majesty and the Queen might be in peril.

The Imperial Ambassador, Simon Renard, writing to Philip of Spain in February 1555.

ACTIVITY

Read Source BB.

1   What is Renard's view of the burnings?

2   Renard did not speak English and did not attend the burnings; how might this affect the reliability of his account?

Source

CC Renard's views appear to be confirmed by John Foxe in his *Acts and Monuments*, written in 1563, during the reign of Elizabeth, when Protestantism was the official religion and Mary Tudor's reputation was being blackened:

Taylor [a local Protestant preacher and teacher] was brought to Hadleigh bridge, where a poor man with five children stood. They held up their hands, and he said, 'O dear father and good shepherd, Dr Taylor, God help you, just as you have often helped me and my poor children!' The streets were full on both sides with men and women of the town and country who waited to see and bless him. When they saw his reverend and ancient face, with a long white beard, they wept and cried out 'God save you, good Dr Taylor!'

ACTIVITY

1   Foxe was an exiled Protestant, highly critical of Mary's policy. He did not witness the burning. How does this affect the reliability of Source CC?

2   Why do you think Foxe wrote an account of all those whom Mary burnt? How might this affect the reliability of his work?

3   Compare Sources BB and CC as evidence for people's reaction to the Marian persecutions.

It must be remembered that burnings were public spectacles. They frequently drew large crowds, but there is little evidence of any being converted. It must also be remembered that the burnings would not have taken place if the local authorities had not enforced the laws. Modern historians offer a slightly different perspective:

Sources

DD *The persecution of Protestants was not a success; nor was it a disaster. If it did not help the Catholic cause, it did not do much to harm it. The burnings were heavily concentrated in the south-east. Protestants were horrified, many committed Catholics approved, and the rest watched curiously as the law took its course.*

Christopher Haigh (1993) *English Reformations*. Oxford University Press.

EE *Persecution did not eliminate heresy; and scattered congregations of Protestants met in many places. London was the safest haven for them in spite of the presence of central government, and reformers assembled there on board ship, in taverns, in the fields, in prisons, and in private houses. But the Protestant clergy, the leaders of their Church, were either executed or exiled; the faithful in England were often led by laymen.*

P. Williams (1995) *The Later Tudors*. Oxford University Press.

How successful was Mary in restoring Catholicism in the localities?

It is difficult to assess the beliefs of the bulk of the population at any time in this period. It is much easier to follow the pattern of official doctrine through the laws, statutes and proclamations that were issued, but they do not tell us what ordinary people felt and whether religious legislation was put into practice. Regional studies have suggested that Catholicism was stronger in the north and west, while Protestantism had made more headway around London and East Anglia. How far does the evidence support this view?

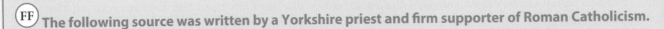

Stretch and challenge

Compare the views put forward in Sources DD and EE on the impact of the Marian persecutions. (Note that you will not be asked to compare the views of two modern historians in the exam.)

Source

(FF) **The following source was written by a Yorkshire priest and firm supporter of Roman Catholicism.**

From August 1553 in many places in Yorkshire, priests were very glad to say mass in Latin, according to the fervent zeal and love they had unto God and his laws. Holy bread and water was given, altars were rebuilt, pictures and images set up once more. The English service was voluntarily laid aside and the Latin taken up again, and all without compulsion of any act or law, but merely on the wish of Queen Mary. And all the old ceremonies were used regularly, once the Lord Cardinal Pole arrived in this realm in November 1554.

ACTIVITY

1   What does Source FF tell you about the progress of the restoration of Catholicism? How swiftly were Catholic practices restored?

2   What are the limitations of this source as evidence for the restoration of Catholicism in England?

Source

(GG) **Although it might be expected that the restoration of Catholic practices in the north would be relatively quick and easy, the following extract from the churchwarden's accounts of Stanford-in-the-Vale, Berkshire, offers a view about progress in the southern counties.**

1553   *Payment to the stonemason for setting up again the high altar.*

1554   *Payment to Henry Snodman to remove a table which served in the church for the communion in the wicked time of the schism.*

1555   *Payment to Edward Whayne for mending the clergyman's robes.*

1556   *Payment to attend the church inspection of my Lord Cardinal Pole. Payment in Abingdon for buying images. Payment for writing an answer to certain questions concerning Religion circulated by my Lord Cardinal Pole to certain of the clergy and Justices of the Peace.*

ACTIVITY

1 What impression does Source GG give of the speed of the restoration of Catholic practices?

2 How far do the churchwarden's accounts agree with the view put forward in Source FF?

3 Do you think Source FF or Source GG is more reliable as evidence for the restoration of Catholicism in England? Why?

Source

HH **An account from the officials of parish churches in Canterbury diocese, a centre of Protestantism, in 1557 offers a different perspective about the implementation of Catholicism.**

Goodnestone Church

*To provide front **cloths** for the altar for holy days, and a **canopy** and **veil** for Lent.*

To make a new lock for the font.

The Chapel of Well, in Ickham

The Chapel is utterly decayed; the two bells are taken away, by whom it is not certainly known.

Goudhurst Church

To provide two decent banners before Rogation week. To repair the chancel ceiling, and the glass windows of the church.

ACTIVITY

1 What does Source HH tell us about the progress of the Marian restoration?

2 Compare Sources GG and HH as evidence for the restoration of Catholicism.

3 Using Sources FF, GG and HH, say what conclusions can be made about the restoration of Catholicism in England under Mary.

cloths, canopy, veil

The altar would have special cloths decorating it on Holy Days, but during Lent it would be covered by a veil, as this was a time of mourning.

By 1558, Mary appeared to have been largely successful in restoring England to the Catholic faith. Her success is a clear indication of the limited success of the Protestant Reformation under Edward and supports the view that the triumph of Protestantism was anything but certain. Mary had restored Catholicism to a largely willing nation. The papacy had been restored and Catholic ceremonies, rituals and ornaments returned. There were also some Catholic reforms with the Westminster Synod. Although legally England was a Catholic country on Mary's death, it is difficult to assess the state of religious belief in the countryside. Religious legislation was not always enforced, and even where it was, people often just conformed, rather than embracing the changes. This view is confirmed by a study of the West Country, a supposedly conservative area, which found there was little support for Protestantism, but just as importantly, there was little enthusiasm for Catholicism. If this is true for the whole country, it would suggest that apathy or indifference had replaced religious zeal.

How successfully did the Elizabethan Religious Settlement solve the religious problems by 1569?

When Elizabeth came to the throne there was much debate as to the direction her religious policy would take. As the last section suggested, she inherited a kingdom that was legally Catholic. However, as the daughter of Anne Boleyn and the product of the break with Rome, it was likely that she would want to take a more Protestant direction. At the same time, many Catholics viewed her as illegitimate and saw Mary Stuart as the rightful heir. The foreign situation also made Elizabeth's position weak; any hasty move towards Protestantism might provoke an invasion from France or Spain, as a religious crusade to restore Catholicism, and might also receive support from Catholics in England.

Source

II **Read the following extract from a report by the Venetian ambassador. He describes the religious confusion apparent in London a few weeks after Elizabeth came to the throne:**

Queen Elizabeth often promised to continue the Catholic religion. But on Christmas Day [1558], Her Majesty told the Bishop that he was not to elevate the host during mass. He replied that this was the only way he knew, so Her Majesty rose and departed. On the same day, two individuals, a mechanic and a cobbler, followed by a very great mob, entered by force in to the church of St Augustine, breaking the locks of the doors. Both leaped into the pulpit and preached, uttering rude jokes about the blessed Queen Mary and Cardinal Pole. Queen Elizabeth forbade such preaching, fearing riots.

This uncertainty continued into 1559, as Source JJ confirms.

Source

JJ **A letter from John Jewel, a Protestant and Bishop of Salisbury, to Peter Martyr, a Protestant theologian who had been Professor of Theology at Oxford during the reign of Edward VI:**

It has happened that the mass has, without the passing of any laws, fallen from use in many places. If the Queen would ban it from her private chapel, the whole thing might easily disappear. She has regulated this mass of hers so that many things are carried out which should not be endured and the mass can be heard without danger. Although the Queen is earnest in the cause of the true religion and desires changes as soon as possible, she cannot be induced to bring about the changes without the effect of law.

ACTIVITY

Compare Sources II and JJ as evidence for the Queen's religious attitude in the first year of her reign.

There is considerable debate about the factors that shaped the Religious Settlement of 1558–59. Some argue that Elizabeth was driven into a more Protestant settlement than she wanted, while others claim that the settlement did not go as far as she would have liked and was restricted by the large number of Catholics in the country. Even after the passing of the Settlement, the challenges did not end, and the years up to 1569 witnessed challenges from both Catholics and **Puritans** to modify or even overthrow the settlement, culminating in the Rebellion of the Northern Earls in 1569 (see Chapter 5).

What factors shaped the Elizabethan Settlement?

In February 1559 three separate bills were introduced into the House of Commons; their aim was to re-establish the monarch as head of the Church and to restore a Protestant form of worship similar to that used under Northumberland. These bills were combined into one and were soon passed by the House of Commons, but the Lords amended them to prevent the restoration of Protestantism. Elizabeth arrested two bishops for disobedience and then introduced a new Supremacy Bill, which made her Supreme Governor rather than Supreme Head. This was an attempt to conciliate Catholics, but there was still a heated debate before it passed the Lords. At the same time, a new uniformity bill, which also gave Catholics concessions, was passed by only three votes in the House of Lords. The struggle to achieve even a moderate settlement showed the problems Elizabeth faced and the strength of Catholicism in Parliament.

> **Puritans**
>
> Protestants who wanted the Church Settlement of 1559 to be more radical. They placed great emphasis on the Bible and preaching. They wanted churches to be plain and the ceremonial aspects of services to be removed.

Source

 Read the following extract from the 1559 Act of Supremacy.

All and every Archbishop, Bishop, and all and every other ecclesiastical person … and all and every temporal judge, justice, mayor, and every other lay or temporal officer and minister and every other person having Your Highness' fee or wages shall make a corporal oath.

I … do utterly testify and declare in my conscience that the Queen's Highness is the only Supreme Governor of this realm and of all other Her Highness' dominions and countries, as well in all spiritual or ecclesiastical things.

ACTIVITY

Read Source KK.

What appears to be the main aim of the Act? Why would Elizabeth be so concerned about this?

Sources

LL **The religious elements of the Act of Uniformity (1559) were very conservative, with the last clause stating:**

That such ornaments of the Church and of the ministers shall be retained and be in use, as was in the Church of England, by the authority of Parliament, in the second year of the reign of King Edward VI.

ACTIVITY

What was the purpose of this part of the Act?

Sources

 An extract from the Prayer Book of 1559:

The body of Our Lord Jesus Christ which was given for thee, preserve thy body and soul unto everlasting life. Take and eat this in remembrance that Christ died for thee and feed on Him in thine heart by faith with thanksgiving. And the minister that delivereth the cup shall say: 'the blood of our Lord Jesus Christ, which was shed for thee, preserve thy body and soul into everlasting life. And drink this in remembrance that Christ's blood was shed for thee and be thankful.'

ACTIVITY

Read Source MM. Compare the view of the Eucharist put forward in Source MM with the view expressed in the First and Second Books of Common Prayer of the reign of Edward VI (Sources L and M on page 75). How do you explain the difference?

Source

NN **If the service and prayer book were conservative in their approach, there was another issue which appeared even more important to the government:**

All and every person and persons inhabiting within this realm ... shall diligently and faithfully, having no lawful or reasonable excuse to be absent, endeavour themselves to resort to their parish church or chapel accustomed upon every Sunday and other days ordained upon pain that every person so offending shall forfeit for every such offence twelve pence to be levied by the church wardens of the Parish.

From the Act of Uniformity, 1559.

ACTIVITY

What, according to Source NN, seems to be the government's main concern? Why would they be concerned about this issue?

Compare the attitude of the governments in Sources NN and BB (page 86) to religious conformity.

The Acts of Supremacy and Uniformity:

- declared Elizabeth Supreme Governor of the Church of England
- restored the religious laws that had been repealed by Mary, taking the Church back to the position of 1552
- removed the Heresy Acts and papal authority
- imposed an oath on all clergy to conform to the new Prayer Book
- introduced punishments for those who did not use the Prayer Book or who objected to its use
- ordered everyone to attend church on Sunday and imposed fines for non-attendance
- ordered the decoration of churches and the dress of the clergy to be as they were in 1549.

The Injunctions of 1559 ordered clergy to:

- uphold the Royal Supremacy
- preach against papal authority
- attack images and relics
- preach only with permission
- report those who did not attend church
- only marry with permission.

Despite attempts to enforce conformity, other problems remained. The Settlement had not resolved the matter of doctrine; this caused confusion and also dismayed many Protestants. The resignation of Catholic bishops and parish clergy meant that Elizabeth was forced to appoint Protestants, but there was a shortage of well-qualified clergymen. Finally, there was the problem of the papacy: it was expected that the Pope would excommunicate Elizabeth, which would have a significant impact on English Catholics, whom Elizabeth had tried to pacify by the moderate settlement. Elizabeth continued to try to win Catholic approval in the early 1560s. The Injunctions of 1559 allowed many of the old vestments to be worn and the communion table to stand where the altar had. In 1560 a Latin edition of the Prayer Book allowed masses for the souls of the dead and in the same year Elizabeth restored a crucifix and candles to the altar in her chapel. The following year she also tried to ban clerical marriage, but compromised and sent away the wives and children of higher clergy.

Stretch and challenge

Compare the views of the two historians below about the success of the Settlement.

From this story of confusion and changing direction emerged a Church which has never subsequently dared define its identity decisively as Protestant or Catholic and which has decided in the end that this is a virtue rather than a handicap.

D. MacCulloch (1990) *The Later Reformation in Tudor England*. Macmillan.

By the time Parliament had closed in mid-May 1559, the Elizabethan Religious Settlement had taken its permanent form. Not everyone was satisfied with it however, the Catholics could hardly like it, although they were not to be seriously persecuted under the new laws. Moreover they were confused. The Pope failed to make it clear to English Catholics where their duty lay. This gentleness towards the Catholics and the Queen's preference for more traditional ornaments in her churches was already worrying some leaders of her new Church, who feared that the new religion would be laxly enforced.

C. Haigh (1984) *The Reign of Elizabeth I*. Longman.

(Note that you will not be asked to compare two secondary sources in the exam.)

ACTIVITY

Which group, Catholic or Protestant, do you think was more satisfied with the Settlement? Why?

How successfully was the Settlement upheld?

The only significant development to the Settlement came in 1563 with the Thirty-Nine Articles. This did move the doctrine of the Church in a more Protestant direction, but there was a great deal of local variation in its implementation.

> ### Source
>
> **Read this historian's comments on the implementation of the Thirty-Nine Articles.**
>
> *The commissioners appointed to enforce the Settlement through royal visitations, reported examples of parish churches which emphasised the ceremonial aspects of the Prayer Book, the singing of hymns accompanied by an organ, and kneeling to receive the bread and wine from a minister wearing full vestments at communion. In other parishes, ministers wore no vestments, there was no music and the bread and wine was received sitting or standing.*
>
> B. Mervyn (2001) *The Reign of Elizabeth*. John Murray.

> ### ACTIVITY
>
> Compare the difficulties outlined in Source OO with those facing Edward and Mary on pages 79–89..

> ### Source
>
> **Now read the following extract from Haigh's *English Reformations*:**
>
> *Parishes held on to mass equipment for as long as they could, or as long as there seemed any chance it might be needed. The surviving churchwarden's accounts suggest that about half of the parishes kept their vestments and mass utensils for at least a decade. Some traded in Catholic chalices for Protestant **communion cups** early in the reign, such as Betrysden in Kent in 1561 and St Andrew's, Canterbury in 1562, perhaps in response to pressure from the Archbishop. There were campaigns to enforce such exchanges in the archdeaconry of Essex in 1564, and in the dioceses of Winchester and Norwich in 1567; at least 275 Norfolk churches bought new communion cups in 1567–68. But many parishes had to be harried into obedience, and at the 1569 visitation of Norfolk thirty-nine were presented for their failure to comply fully.*
>
> Christopher Haigh (1993) *English Reformations*. Oxford University Press.

communion cup

A goblet in which members of the congregation would receive the wine at the Eucharist.

> ### ACTIVITY
>
> 1 What is Haigh's view of the success of the Elizabethan Settlement?
>
> 2 What does this tell us about the religious views of many people in England?

> ### Stretch and challenge
>
> Compare Source PP with those for Mary's reign (pages 88–89) about the success of implementing religious change.

Elizabeth adopted a tolerant approach towards the implementation of the Settlement. In Lancashire, a strongly Catholic county, only 12 clergy were deprived of their **livings**. At the same time, the nobility were not required to take the Oath of Supremacy and when, in 1563, it became law that a second refusal would result in the death penalty, Elizabeth insisted that no one should be asked to take the oath twice. The enforcement of the Settlement would depend heavily upon the willingness of **Justices of the Peace** to enforce the laws on church attendance. In many areas they were unwilling, either because they were Catholics themselves or because they did not want to persecute friends or people of a similar social status. As a consequence many people were able to carry on their traditional religious practices unaffected. Despite this moderate approach, many Catholics were uneasy about Elizabeth's claim to be Supreme Governor, and as the regime began to appoint more Protestant clergy and bishops, so it resulted in the Northern Earls' Rebellion in 1569 (see Chapter 5).

> **living**
> A church office which brought its occupier an income.

Source

(QQ) **An extract from the visitation to the diocese of Chichester in 1569:**

Many churches there have no sermons, not one in seven years, and some not one in twelve years. Except in the area around Lewes and a little in Chichester, the whole diocese is very blind and superstitious because of the lack of teaching.

(QQ) **This account of the changes carried out in parish churches was written by an Elizabethan chronicler, William Harrison, in 1564:**

There used to be a great partition between the choir and the main body of the church, but it is now either very small or has gone, and to tell the truth, it is not necessary. The minister says the service in the main body of the church facing the congregation. By this, the ignorant learn various Psalms and the common prayers by heart and those that can read do pray together with the vicar.

ACTIVITY
Read Sources QQ and RR.

1. What is the message of Source QQ?

2. How useful is Source QQ in explaining the success of the Elizabethan Reformation at the end of the period?

3. How useful is Source RR in explaining the success of the religious changes under Elizabeth?

4. Compare these two sources as evidence for the implementation of the Elizabethan Settlement.

> **Justices of the Peace**
> Magistrates whose job it was to see that the laws were obeyed in their area. They were appointed for every district and as the century progressed their responsibilities increased. Most of them were members of the gentry.

If the aim of the religious settlement was to avoid conflict and achieve political stability, it is clear that it was a success. Elizabeth did not face the religious unrest that was a feature of mid-sixteenth-century France or the Netherlands. A state Church was established which allowed Elizabeth to deal with religious opponents in the same way as political ones, using the treason laws and therefore avoiding the mistake of creating religious martyrs. The Church was also able to consolidate its religious position. A broadly based, national Church

was established. The Thirty-Nine Articles, 1563, clearly set out Protestant beliefs, such as Predestination, without attacking Catholic beliefs. However, despite these successes, it did not satisfy devout Catholics or Puritans.

Despite this, the settlement survived, largely unchallenged, until 1569. The arrival of Mary Queen of Scots was probably the trigger for the crisis. Elizabeth's opponents saw in her a potential leader and figure around whom plots and rebellion could develop. In the eyes of many Catholics she was the legitimate ruler, as they viewed Henry's marriage to Anne Boleyn as illegal. Many Catholics were also unhappy about Elizabeth's claim to be Supreme Governor, and as the regime began to appoint more Protestant clergy and bishops so unrest grew, culminating in the Northern Rebellion of 1569 (see Chapter 5).

Conclusion

It is difficult to assess the impact of the religious changes. Chapter 5 will suggest that religion played at least a contributory role in four major rebellions: the Pilgrimage of Grace in 1536, the Western Rebellion of 1549, the attempt by Northumberland to stop Mary taking the throne in 1553 and the Northern Rebellion of 1569. Therefore, it could be argued that religion contributed to potential crises. However, although there were extremists on both sides, the majority of the population were moderate and willing to accept whatever doctrine was held by the ruling elite. Therefore, it might be suggested that the religious changes had less impact on the population than was once thought. There appears to have been little antagonism between Catholics and Protestants, and this was the basis for the religious compromise that prevented England from subsiding into the religious wars that characterised much of sixteenth-century Europe. It was only under Mary Tudor's regime that religious persecution was extensive, but even that pales into insignificance when compared with events on the continent. It is therefore perhaps fair to conclude that the moderation of many of the changes is the best explanation for the lack of religious instability in the period 1536–69.

What were the effects of social and economic change in the period 1536–69?

4

This chapter will consider six main questions:

- What were the main social and economic developments of the period?
- What were the causes of the price rise?
- What were the effects of the agrarian changes?
- What were the effects of poverty and how did the government deal with the problem?
- Why did the cloth trade decline and how did the government deal with it?
- How serious an issue were disease and famine in the period?

This chapter will also help to develop your source skills by encouraging you to group sources and assess how far they support a particular view by evaluating their provenance and using the knowledge you will have gained from this chapter.

What were the main social and economic developments of the period?

For modern historians, two developments stand out. The first is the price rise, which affected all sectors of society from the monarch to the lowest labourer and was regularly commented on by contemporaries. The second, closely linked to the first, is the dramatic rise in the population, though this was hardly noticed by contemporaries. In studying this latter development we have to be aware that there are many difficulties, chiefly the lack of statistical information available.

Because of this lack of information, we have to work within an area of uncertainty. Historians try to calculate the population using local sources, including wills, to get an idea of the size of families; they also use tax records and family Bibles, which often contain a record of family ownership. Despite the problem with sources, the scale and nature of the price rise supports the generally accepted view that this period witnessed a substantial population increase, which would put enormous pressure on food supplies and contribute to the inflation that characterised this period.

This view is supported by the following:

- Agricultural prices went up faster than the prices of industrial goods, which is what we would expect if a growing population was putting pressure on food supplies.
- Grain prices went up faster than meat, dairy or wool prices, which is again to be expected if the population was rising.

The population of England had been rising at the start of the fourteenth century, possibly reaching 6 million, but the **Black Death** and other outbreaks of plague ended this period of growth. It was not until 1470 that numbers began to recover, and it is estimated that by 1520 the population had reached 2.3 million.

Black Death

The bubonic plague arrived in England in 1349. It was carried by rats on ships, and killed somewhere in the region of 30 per cent of the population.

4 What were the effects of social and economic change in the period 1536–69?

Year	Population (millions)
1536	2.7
1541	2.8
1546	2.9
1551	3.0
1556	3.2
1561	3.0
1566	3.1
1571	3.2

Table 4.1 An estimate of population rise in England in the mid-sixteenth century. (Adapted from Anderson and Imperator (2001) *An Introduction to Tudor England*. Hodder.)

ACTIVITY

1   What do you notice about the growth of the population throughout the period?

2   What reasons do you think there are to explain the pattern?

English sweat

A form of influenza.

Historians have debated whether the cause of the rise was a decline in death rates or a rise in fertility rates, or even a combination of both. Those who have argued for a decline in death rates have suggested that the plague, the great killer of earlier periods, became less frequent and less intense. However, it should be remembered that in the mid-sixteenth century a new disease, usually called the **English sweat**, hit the country and may have reduced the population by 6 per cent, especially in the crowded and unsanitary towns. On the other hand, historians who have argued for an increase in fertility rates have suggested that increasing prosperity earlier in the period, linked to a series of good harvests, encouraged people to marry younger. As a result, women spent more of their married life in child-bearing age and therefore were more likely to have larger families. However, harvests were not always good and an increase in the number of mouths to feed would lead to a decrease in prosperity. This has led some to challenge the view that people would marry younger, and to believe that early marriage would have been discouraged.

Whatever the cause of this population rise, it resulted in a younger population, which would have an impact on production and consumption levels. A younger population meant that although there were more mouths to feed, there were fewer adults to produce the food. This created an increased demand for food, and historians have calculated that the Early Modern economy was able to grow at only 0.5 per cent per year, whereas population was growing at 1 per cent per year, so demand was outstripping supply and therefore pushing prices up.

If contemporaries were unaware, until the end of the period, of the growth in population, they were in no doubt about the scale of the price rise. However they differed about the causes, and these will be examined in the next section.

How great was the price rise?

The index of prices on the next page shows the average price of (1) the foodstuffs that might have formed the diet of a building worker in the south of England and (2) a sample of industrial products.

Average for each decade	Foodstuffs (%)	Industrial products (%)
1491–1500	100	97
1501–10	106	98
1511–20	116	102
1521–30	159	110
1531–40	161	110
1541–50	217	127
1551–60	315	186
1561–70	298	218
1571–80	341	223

Table 4.2   Index of prices in the sixteenth century. (From E.H. Phelps-Brown and S.V. Hopkins (1962) 'Seven Centuries of the Prices of Consumables', in *Essays in Economic History*, Arnold.)

ACTIVITY

Look at Table 4.2.

1   What do you notice about the speed at which at the index for foodstuffs rises, compared with industrial goods?

2   Why might this occur?

3   Which decade sees the greatest rise in the index for foodstuffs and industrial goods?

4   Compare these figures with those in Table 4.1. What do you notice? What does this suggest about the population rise and price rise?

There are problems in using sources like Table 4.2. The main problem is that prices, wages and even rents varied across the country. The price of foodstuffs outlined in Table 4.2 for a building worker in the south-east may not have applied to other types of workers in other areas of the country. Just as importantly, these figures fail to take account of whether the individual had access to land. In most areas, all but the poorest would have access to some land, at least in the form of gardens or orchards. Even when this was not available, people had the right of entry onto the **common land**, which would provide some food, heating and building material, and enabled most of the population to escape the full force of the price rise. This is why the loss of common land through enclosure was such an important issue (see pages 107–108). We also do not know whether the labourer in Table 4.2 would also have received any food or ale as part of his wages, which would again have shielded him from the full impact of the rise. Against this must be balanced the fact that building work may have been seasonal, so that many workers had to have more than one job. The existence of all these variables makes it difficult for the historian to draw any definite conclusions about the impact of the price rise on the population.

Even so, food prices were important, particularly to the lower orders who lived in towns. The purchase of foodstuffs, particularly grain and bread, may have accounted for two-thirds of their income. The dramatic price rises in this period would have a major impact on the standard of living, as wages were certainly not rising as fast as prices. The population rise itself helped to push down wage levels and reduce the opportunity for employment.

The impact of the rising prices can be seen in the other major social problems of the period: poverty and vagrancy. It can even be seen as a cause of disease and famine. However, there

common land

Village land where everyone who was not a landowner could gather wood and berries and graze their animals.

rack-renting

Making exorbitant increases in the rent on land.

4 What were the effects of social and economic change in the period 1536–69?

forestalling

Buying up goods in order to sell them at a higher price at a later date.

regrating

Buying up commodities in advance so as to sell them later at a much higher price. By buying up the goods the merchant created a shortage and so forced up the price.

were other social problems; the one most commonly commented on by contemporaries was probably enclosure or the loss of common land, which sometimes resulted in riot or even rebellion, as in 1549 (see Chapter 5, pages 131–134).

What were the causes of the price rise?

The most interesting issue when considering the causes of the price rise is to note how far historians and contemporaries disagree about possible causes. Contemporaries, faced with a problem that they could not easily explain, tended to look for scapegoats. Most commonly blamed were greedy landowners who were enclosing or **rack-renting**, and merchants who were **forestalling** or **regrating**. Contemporaries tended to take a moral view of society; they held to the medieval theory of a 'just price', where everything had its appropriate or normal price. If prices went up, then greed was responsible.

Source

A Read the following extract from a sermon preached by Hugh Latimer before Henry VIII in 1539.

*My father was a yeoman [an independent farmer] and had no lands of his own. He rented a farm for £3 or £4 a year at the most; and hereupon he tilled so much as kept half a dozen men. He had room for 100 sheep and my mother milked 30 kine [cows]. He was able to arm himself and his horse for the king. I can remember that I buckled his harness when he went unto **Blackheath Field**. He kept me to school, or else I had not been able to preach before the King's majesty now. He kept hospitality for his poor neighbours and gave some alms to the poor. All this he did of the said farm, whereas the man that now has the farm pays £16 per year, or more, and is not able to do anything for his prince, for himself nor for his children, or give a cup of drink to the poor.*

Source

B The following source was published in 1546 as a pamphlet, appealing to the House of Commons on behalf of the poor. It describes the causes of the social problems.

Many landlords oppress the common people. They have increased their rents, so that they charge £40 rather than 40 shillings [£2] for a new lease, and £5 not 5 nobles [almost £2] for its annual rent, so we now pay more to them than we earn. The result is that many thousands of us who once lived honestly upon our labour must now beg, or borrow, or rob and steal, to get food for our poor wives and children. They also compel others to surrender their rights to hold leases for two or three lives and to accept instead leases for just twenty-one years.

A supplication of the Poore Commons, 1546.

Blackheath Field

The Cornish tax rebels of 1497 reached Blackheath, where they were defeated by a royal army. Latimer's father was a member of the army.

ACTIVITY

Compare Sources A and B as evidence for the changing attitudes of landlords and tenants.

As you read the two sources, think carefully about what appears to have changed between the writing of 1546 and the sermon of 1539. Why might attitudes have changed? Is there anything in the background of the writers that might explain their attitudes? How might this affect the reliability of their writing?

ACTIVITY

1   Who does the writer of Source B blame for the social problems?

2   What does he say this group is doing that harms the ordinary people?

The writings of a group known as **The Commonwealth Men** are the clearest evidence we have to show that contemporaries recognised that the rise in prices was significant. Although historians have disagreed over whether such a group existed, the name has been given to a number of writers, particularly of the 1540s, who were concerned with economic and social welfare. The group included men such as **John Hales**, best known for his work with the Enclosure Commission (pages 108–110), Robert Crowley and Sir Thomas Smith. A number of Protestant preachers, such as Hugh Latimer, were concerned with the plight of the poor and sought to offer solutions. They usually adopted a moralistic tone, as in Latimer's comment, 'You landlords, you rent-raisers.' The Catholic Church also took a moralistic approach, blaming the price rise on moneylenders.

The Commonwealth Men

A group of humanist intellectuals who argued that the wealthy had some obligation to help the poor. It used to be argued that they influenced Somerset's social policy.

Source

C The most famous writing of the period was Sir Thomas Smith's 'A Discourse of the Common Weal of this Realm of England' which, although it was not published until 1581, was probably written in 1549 and revised in the 1570s. The writing is an imaginary dialogue between various groups in society who put forward their views about the economic problems of the time. In the first draft, Smith blamed debasement, unlike others such as Hales, who blamed enclosure, but in the revised draft he blames:

… the great store and plenty of treasure which is walking in these parts of the world, far more in these our days than ever our forefathers have seen in times past. Who doth not understand of the infinite sums of gold and silver which are gathered from the Indies and other countries, and so yearly transported unto these coasts.

ACTIVITY

Read Source C.

In what ways and why has Smith's interpretation of the causes of the price rise changed from his first draft?

debasement

A reduction in the silver content of the coinage and its replacement with a cheaper metal. This yielded enough silver to enable the government to mint more money.

BIOGRAPHY

Sir John Hales

Hales became famous in 1548 for leading the Enclosure Commission established by Somerset. He was a member of the Commonwealth Men and had sympathy for the poor.

4 What were the effects of social and economic change in the period 1536–69?

Contemporaries stressed the greed of landlords, debasement, enclosure and the influx of foreign bullion as the major causes of the price rise, but there are other possible reasons. What are the other reasons, and how far does the evidence support or challenge them?

The following arguments need to be considered as possible causes of the price rise:

- debasement
- bullion (the gold and silver that arrived from the Spanish Empire in the Americas)
- war
- bad harvests
- land sales.

Debasement

Arguments in favour

- Debasement took place between 1542 and 1551, which coincides with the period of the rapid mid-century price rise.
- By reducing the amount of silver content the government was able to increase the amount of money in circulation, so there was more money chasing the same quantity of goods, forcing up prices as supply could not meet demand.
- The public knew that there was less silver in the coins, therefore sellers simply demanded more money.

Arguments against

- Inflation had started well before debasement began.
- Inflation continued after Northumberland reduced the money supply in 1551, and the same was true under Elizabeth.
- Inflation was happening throughout Europe, therefore the actions of the English government are not sufficient to explain the development.

Bullion

Arguments in favour

- The output of the silver mines in central Europe increased fivefold between 1460 and 1530, which allowed governments to mint more money.
- There was much silver entering England from Spain during Elizabeth's reign. Trade between the two nations continued despite war, and English privateers also brought back large quantities.

Arguments against

- The main influx of silver, which came from the Spanish mines in the New World, particularly Potosí in Bolivia, came in the period after 1545, and this is too late to account for the inflation of the earlier period.
- It is unlikely that enough silver reached England from Spain to account for the rapid inflation. It was only in the latter decades of Elizabeth's reign that privateers were capturing significant amounts, and this was well after rapid inflation had started.

War

Arguments in favour

- Heavy government spending during times of war increased demand and would therefore create inflation.
- War forced England to borrow money to feed and clothe the army and build defences.
- Inflation started when Henry VII's more peaceful reign ended and Henry VIII's aggressive policies began.
- The 1540s, when inflation was at its greatest, were the years of heavy military spending.

Arguments against

- Government spending in the Tudor period, even in times of war, was not as high as modern standards and therefore the impact on inflation would have been minimal.

Bad harvests

Arguments in favour

- Crop failures reduced the amount of food available and forced prices up.
- The 1540s saw a large number of poor or very poor harvests.

Arguments against

- Bad harvests would cause only a temporary shortage; therefore it is difficult to see how this would explain the continuous price rise of the sixteenth century.
- If the cause was just bad harvests, why did the price of industrial goods rise?

Land sales

Arguments in favour

- There was more land available to purchase, particularly after the dissolution of the monasteries (see Chapter 3, page 64).
- Increased demand for land among the gentry and the merchants forced prices up.

Arguments against

- Although the increased availability of land coincides with the start of the period of inflation and would also have had an impact on rents, land sales affected very few. Land sales would not have an impact on the wide range of goods that rose in price.

Source

D A clergyman identifies some major economic grievances. The author had been chaplain to Protector Somerset.

See how rich men, especially sheep owners, oppress the King's subjects by enclosing the common pasture and filling it with their sheep. How many sheep they have! Yet when was wool so expensive, or mutton so great a price? If this goes on, the people will die of cold or starve to death. For these greedy wolves will either sell their wool and their sheep at their own high price, or else not at all. Other men buy up houses, even whole villages, and then allow them to fall into ruin and decay.

Thomas Becon, *The Jewel of Joy*, 1547–48

E The economic problems of the time are discussed in an imaginary dialogue between a small farmer, a merchant and a knight.

Small farmer: *These enclosures ruin us all, for they make us pay more for our land so we have no money to put to ploughing.*

Merchant: *There is a shortage of all things which we grow in this land or which we buy from overseas, and food is more expensive. If enclosures are the cause, then they should be removed.*

Knight: *Enclosures cannot be the cause of the shortage of cattle, for enclosures encourage and protect cattle. All things are more expensive now, but you can raise the price of the goods you sell, whereas we gentlemen have nothing to sell and yet have to pay higher prices.*

Sir Thomas Smith, *A Discourse of the Common Weal of this Realm of England*, 1549.

F A leading Protestant comments on the causes of recent unrest across much of England in 1549 (see Chapter 5).

You preachers, I urge you to speak against greed, and criticise those great men and men of power, who oppress the poor. For greed is the cause of rebellion. Greed was the cause of rebellion last year, by both gentlemen and common people. The people thought they had the right to things they desired. The gentlemen wanted to keep what they had, so they rebelled or disobeyed the King's orders. Thus both sides were greedy, and both sides rebelled.

Hugh Latimer, sermon, preached in 1550.

G One of the Commonwealth writers attacks landlords for their grasping behaviour and a lack of obedience to the Crown in 1548–49.

Contrary to the law against oppression and extortion, you have enclosed from the poor their common land, levied greater entry fees payable on new leases, excluded them from their rightful use of the common land, and raised their rents. What obedience did you show when the King's proclamations were sent forth to open up your enclosures, and yet you continued to enclose? If you loved your country, would you not have prevented the recent great destruction which followed from your incurable greed?

Robert Crowley, *The Way to Wealth*, 1550.

H A modern historian notes some key economic and social problems of the period.

The government was faced by difficult economic and social problems. Population, and with it inflation, was still rising. In 1550 the Antwerp cloth market finally collapsed, causing widespread unemployment among textile workers. The debasement of the coinage yet again in 1550–1 raised inflation still further. Grain prices rose rapidly, a situation worsened by harvest failures.

Nigel Heard (1990) *Edward VI and Mary: a Mid-Tudor Crisis?* Hodder.

ACTIVITY

Read Sources D–H on the causes of the price rise and the associated social problems and answer the following question (there is guidance below to help you).

Using your own knowledge, assess the interpretation that the main cause of the social problems of the period was the greed of the landlords.

Examiner's advice

You must remember that this is a source paper and you should not simply write an essay about the social problems of the period. Most of the marks available are for using the sources and evaluating them to answer the question. The sources must be evaluated, not simply used to illustrate a point, if you want to achieve the higher levels – therefore avoid writing 'Source E says…'. Also avoid simply going through each source and paraphrasing it.

On the positive side you must, having evaluated all the sources, reach a judgement – the examiner wants to know whether you think the greed of the landlords was the main cause of the social problems. If you think it was, you should have explained why. Alternatively, if you think there is a better explanation, you should have explained why greed is not the most important and why the other cause is a better explanation.

Remember, you have already developed evaluation skills when comparing sources as evidence. You should not forget these skills for this question.

- Have you considered the **origin or author** of the source and how it might affect reliability?
- Have you considered the **purpose** of the source and how it might affect reliability?
- Have you looked at the **date** of the source and how it might affect reliability?

The new skill in this chapter is to use your own **knowledge of the topic** to evaluate the source.

What do you know that either agrees or disagrees with what is said in the source? If you have knowledge that supports the interpretation in the sources, it is likely to make the source more reliable. On the other hand, if you have knowledge that disagrees with the interpretation in the source, it is likely to make the source less reliable. Do remember, however, that you may have knowledge that agrees with part of the source and disagrees with other parts.

The table below should help you to reach the higher levels as it will encourage you to group the sources and ascribe a relative value to each one. It is important to fill in both the 'for' and 'against' columns if the evidence justifies it, so that you see that sources can support different interpretations. Remember: Bands 1 and 2 are awarded to those answers with a considerable focus on the 'evaluation' column.

Source	Evaluation. How useful is it? How reliable is it?	For the interpretation because:	Against the interpretation because:
D			
E			
F			
G			
H			

4 What were the effects of social and economic change in the period 1536–69?

What were the effects of the agrarian changes?

There were a number of agricultural problems in the period. This is clearly shown by an Act of Parliament in 1534 which limited to 2000 the number of sheep one person could own.

Source

I Read the following extract from the Act of Parliament limiting the number of sheep one person could own.

Various people of this realm, to whom God has given great abundance of wealth, have lately invented ways to gather together into few hands a great number of farms, great plenty of cattle, especially sheep. They put such lands as they can get to pasture and not to tillage. As a result they have not only pulled down churches and towns and raised the rents of their lands, or charged excessively fines that no poor man is able to pay, but also have raised the prices of corn, cattle, wool, pigs, geese, hens, eggs etc. almost double above the customary prices. Now a multitude of people of this realm are not able to provide meat, drink and clothes necessary for themselves, their wives and children and are so discouraged with poverty that they fall daily to theft or pitifully die of hunger and cold.

ACTIVITY

Read Source I.

1. What agricultural problems does the Act identify?

2. What does the Act see as the consequences of these problems?

3. How useful is the Act as evidence of the effects agricultural change?

If the Act was correct in its assumptions then this was a serious problem, as over 90 per cent of the population lived off the land. For much of the time, they produced enough to survive on, and in years of good harvests there might be a small surplus that could be sold to purchase luxuries. However, in a bad year there was the prospect of starvation. Overall, the agricultural system was able to feed the population and evidence of starvation in this period is rare.

ACTIVITY

Study Figure 4.1, which shows the quality of English harvests in the period, and answer the following questions.

1. Did England have good rather than poor harvests in the period 1536–69?

2. Are there any periods where there is a succession of bad harvests? What do you think the impact would be?

3. Why might there be a strong connection between a bad harvest and outbreaks of disorder?

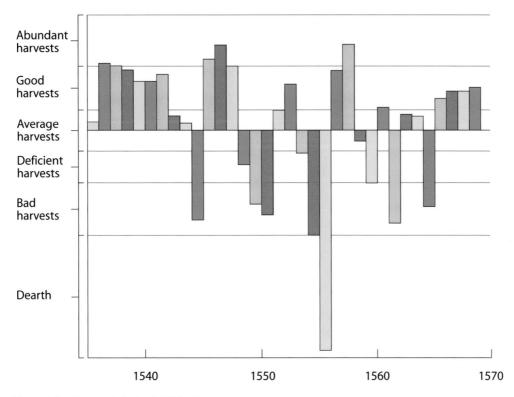

Figure 4.1   Harvests in England, 1536–69

The most controversial effects of agrarian changes were caused by enclosure. It is important that you have a clear understanding of what is meant by the term and also that you realise that there was both good and bad enclosure. Enclosure did mean an end to the old open-field system, where each peasant had the right to farm small strips of land that were scattered throughout the village. Peasants also had the right to graze animals on the common land. This land was available to all non-landowners; it was usually unfenced and underwent little supervision. The old system was not very efficient as about one-third of all land had to be left fallow each year to allow it to recover. However, the increasing population and rising prices encouraged landowners to look to make even greater profits from their land. Most importantly, the growing profits to be made from sheep-farming encouraged enclosure.

As suggested above, there were various types of enclosure:

■ The first was where the landowner simply put a fence around his land to protect his crops and animals and allow him to farm more effectively. This had little impact on other villagers and would cause little concern.

■ Where a landowner's lands were spread out across the village he might try to consolidate them. This could be achieved in a friendly way by exchanging land with other landowners, and again would cause little concern. On the other hand, it might involve legal threats or financial pressures, which could cause disquiet. This process of consolidating land was known as **engrossing**.

■ The landowner might find a way of taking the common land and denying its use to other villagers. This was the most common cause of disquiet and was often the signal for unrest.

engrossing

The redistribution of small pieces of land so that the landowner could have all of his land together in one place.

It was not just the enclosing that caused disquiet; much depended upon how the land was used. As result of consolidating his land, the landowner might find that he needed fewer labourers than in the past, which would result in unemployment, or he might decide to turn his newly enclosed land over to sheep-runs, which would require far less labour than arable farming.

Source

J Even contemporaries were able to distinguish between good and bad enclosure, as is made clear by this comment from John Hales in 1548.

But first, to declare unto you what is meant by this word enclosures. It is not taken when a man encloses and hedges in his own proper ground, where no man has common rights. For such enclosure is very beneficial to the commonwealth; it is a cause of great increase of wood: but it is meant thereby, when any man has taken away and enclosed any other men's common land, or has pulled down houses of husbandry, and converted the lands from tillage to pasture. This is the meaning of this word, and so we pray you to remember it.

John Hales, *Instructions to the Enclosure Commission*, 1548

ACTIVITY

Using pages 106–108, ensure that you have a clear understanding of the following terms:

- enclosure
- common land
- engrossing
- open-field system.

The enclosure of common land was likely to provoke the fiercest response from villagers. They claimed that they had customary right of access to the common land and that it was vital for their survival, particularly in times of rising prices and poor harvests. They were able to pasture their animals there, cut timber or peat, and fish and hunt. As a result the common land provided a supplement for food and allowed peasants to keep animals that would feed them.

It is therefore not surprising that the reaction to enclosure could be violent. Villagers often tore down fences or drew up petitions and embarked on law suits. It was the enclosure of land that was the trigger for Kett's Rebellion in 1549 (see Chapter 5, pages 133–135), and in 1548 at Northaw in Hertfordshire, the locals blew up the rabbit warren that the local landowner had established on the common land. It is therefore hardly surprising that throughout this period the government was opposed to the policy of enclosure, seeing it as a threat to order.

The following action was taken during the Tudor period:

1515 Acts were passed ordering the return of pastureland to arable use where crop production was a traditional method of farming.

1534 An Act was passed forbidding anyone to own more than 2000 sheep or have more than two farms, except in their own parish.

1536 Cromwell introduced an Act to stop enclosing.

1548 Enclosure Commission established under John Hales.

1551 An Act against enclosures appointed a commission to seek out offenders.

1563 An Act ordered that all land used for crops for at least four of the last 35 years must remain arable. The Act also forbade further conversions from arable to sheep farming.

Why did landlords enclose?

- The Black Death had caused a decline in the population and consequently there was a labour shortage.
- The shortage of labour encouraged some landlords to turn to sheep-farming.
- Sheep-farming was encouraged by the rising demand for woollen cloth, both to supply the increasing population at home and for the overseas market. As a result, there was a ready market for landlords who converted from arable to pasture.
- Pasture or sheep-farming had lower overheads and therefore allowed landowners to increase their profits.
- Sheep-farming required fewer labourers and therefore landowners spent less on wages.
- The increase in demand for food, with the rising population, did encourage some landowners to enclose so that they could follow intensive methods of farming.

Why was enclosure disliked?

- The enclosure of common land meant that many peasants lost their common rights and therefore their ability to graze their livestock.
- Enclosure was often accompanied by rack-renting, where rents could be adjusted depending on the economic situation.
- Enclosure was seen by contemporaries as the cause of all the social problems of the time: unemployment, as fewer labourers were required; vagrancy, as there were fewer jobs; increased unrest as a result of all factors.
- **Tenants-at-will** and **copyholders** had no legal claim to the land they rented and therefore could be either evicted or faced with a rent rise they could not afford.
- Evicted tenants were often unable to find other work in the village and therefore moved to the towns to look for work.
- The drift to the towns created a large number of **vagrants** who were a concern to the authorities. It also resulted in a significant increase in the number of urban poor.
- Conversion from arable farming to pasture was opposed because it was believed that shepherds made poorer soldiers than ploughmen. It was also believed that depopulation would weaken the nation's defences as it would endanger contributions to the **militia**.

The authorities had idealistic motives: they wanted to maintain the social structure and this involved protecting peasants as well as landowners. Therefore, it is not surprising that preachers such as Hugh Latimer, and laymen such as John Hales, denounced greedy landlords.

Enclosure led to popular unrest. It played a role in the Pilgrimage of Grace, the Western Rebellion and Kett's Rebellion (see Chapter 5). It was therefore a major concern to the authorities.

tenants-at-will
Occupants of land who had no rights and could be forced off it at the will of the landowner.

copyholders
Landowners who leased their land over a long period and could pass it on to their children.

vagrants
The wandering poor, who roamed the country either looking for work or, as the government believed, causing unrest.

militia
Local forces made up of commoners. They were not professional soldiers, but were required to train for a number of days per year.

Despite the large number of complaints about enclosure, it must be remembered that between 1500 and 1600 only 2 per cent of land was enclosed. Even in areas where there was substantial enclosure, it is estimated that no more than 9 per cent of land was enclosed. Historians also acknowledge that there was no large-scale depopulation of villages in the period. More recent work has suggested that after 1550, enclosures were carried out not to create large sheep runs, but to increase the efficiency of arable farming as corn was now more profitable than sheep (this was because of the increased demand created by the rising population). As a result, contemporaries probably over-exaggerated the impact of enclosure, although it would be fair to say that the impact varied from region to region and from individual to individual.

ACTIVITY

Read Sources J (page 108) and K–N below, on the impact of enclosure, then answer the following question.

Using your own knowledge, assess the interpretation that enclosure caused more harm than good.

Sources

(K) Extracts from the demands of the rebels in East Anglia, 1549.

We pray your grace that no lord of the manor shall graze sheep on the commons.

We pray that it is not lawful for the lords of the manor to purchase lands freehold and let them out copyhold to their great advantage and to the undoing of your poor subjects.

We pray that no lord, knight, squire or gentleman grazes or feeds any bullocks or sheep if he has an income of forty pounds per year from his lands, except to provide for his house.

(L) The head of the Enclosure Commission explains his view of the recent unrest. The Enclosure Commission was set up by Protector Somerset in 1548 to look into the legality of the enclosing of land.

Was there not, long before this Commission against enclosures was sent forth, a rising in Hertfordshire for the commons at Northaw and Cheshunt? Can it be denied that the first rising this year was in Somerset from where it entered into Gloucestershire and many other places? This was before the places where I was with the Commission were infected with insurrection. And yet, in many places where we were, where the people had just cause of grief and have complained a great many years without remedy, they have been very quiet and showed themselves most humble and obedient subjects.

But if the cause of these seditions for the commons be sought, it shall be well seen that it springs from the greediness of the men who slander me.

Extract from a defence written by John Hales against accusations that the Enclosure Commission had been responsible for the disorder of 1549.

(M) A Protestant clergyman, one of the Commonwealth writers, considers what lay behind the popular rebellions in 1549.

Rebellion is a dangerous disease and its causes must be rooted out. If I should ask a poor man what is the cause of rebellion, he will blame the great farmers, lawyers, gentlemen, knights and lords. Men of greed; men who take our houses from us, and enclose our commons. If I should ask these greedy men what is the cause of rebellion, they will say that the peasants are too wealthy, they are disobedient, they would destroy gentlemen. They will try again to compel the King to grant their requests, and will be punished for it, as happened last year.

Robert Crowley, *The Way to Wealth*, 1550.

> **Sources**
>
> **(N)** A contemporary writer suggests ways to improve agricultural production.
>
> *More plenty of mutton and beef,*
>
> *Corn, butter, and cheese of the best,*
>
> *More wealth anywhere, to be brief,*
>
> *More people, more handsome and willing,*
>
> *Where find ye? Go search any coast,*
>
> *Than there, where enclosure is most.*
>
> Thomas Tusser, *Five Hundred Points of Good **Husbandry**,* 1557.

What were the effects of poverty, and how did the government deal with the problem?

husbandry
The management and farming of the land.

Who were the poor, and how numerous were they?

Some historians have suggested that up to half the population of Tudor England was unable to earn enough money to feed itself. This included those who were incapable of work, such as the very young, the very old and the sick, but there were also others, particularly at times of harvest failure or depressions in the cloth trade, when workers were laid off. Any investigation of who the poor were, or the scale of the problem, is beset by the difficulty of definitions. The listings and censuses available to historians mean that we are dependent on contemporary definitions of poverty, which varied greatly. One of the greatest problems for the authorities was the distinction between the deserving poor (those who were unable to work) and the undeserving poor (those who were capable of working but chose not to). This was much easier to identify in rural areas where the deserving poor were recognised and probably known by the rest of the community. In towns, particularly the larger ones, it was much harder for the authorities to know who was genuinely unable to work.

What is noticeable about poverty in this period is that it was no longer a temporary condition, often associated either with old age, when people were unable to work, or with couples with young families, where the children were consumers, but not producers. The young age of the population was reflected in the fact that many children under the age of ten now lived in poverty, with some censuses suggesting that up to half the children of this age group could be counted as poor. There was also a significant number of single women, either widows or abandoned wives, with some towns recording numbers as high as 25 per cent. However, long-term poverty was a new development and as the numbers grew, so they included more and more ordinary families.

A census carried out by the City Council of Norwich in 1570 gives some indication of the types of people drawn into poverty (some appear in more than one category, hence the overall total is more than 100 per cent):

- 17 per cent came from broken families, particularly where the father was absent
- 25 per cent suffered from either illness or old age
- 42 per cent were unable to work
- 8 per cent had large families
- 17 per cent were unemployed.

Most of the poor in urban areas came from two social groups: unskilled labourers and the urban poor. Unskilled labourers could easily slip into poverty because of poor harvests or a slump in trade, or simply through illness. The urban poor included the unemployed, tenants who had been evicted from their homes in the countryside and had drifted to the towns in search of work, and even ex-servants from the monasteries. This group could be divided into two categories: those who were prepared to work and those who were not.

The scale of the problem also varied annually and geographically. Censuses suggest figures ranging from 5 per cent to 22 per cent. However, it is clear that poverty was at its greatest in towns: a survey of Worcester in 1557 suggested 18 per cent and of Norwich in 1570 suggested 25 per cent (500 men, 850 women and 1000 children). The fact that the censuses measured different things, sometimes those receiving aid, in other instances those in need of relief, makes it difficult to reach any definite conclusions.

It is clear that the authorities were particularly concerned by the growing number of idle or undeserving poor or vagrants, as they were seen as a threat to the social order. This group included former soldiers and sailors who were reduced to begging when they returned from fighting (these were of particular concern as they were often armed). Some vagrants had even turned poverty and begging into a profession, pretending to be insane! Records suggest that the largest component of the idle poor were apprentices and servants. In general, records suggest that most were aged between 15 and 40, which differed considerably from the age of the deserving poor. The idle poor were usually single and male, and covered large distances, with many moving towards the south-east, particularly to London, in search of work. The authorities viewed these as the immoral sector of society, and they were certainly seen as less respectable than unemployed tradesmen wandering with their families looking for work.

What were the causes of poverty?

The population rise

We have already considered the scale of the population rise, but it must be emphasised that a doubling of the population in the sixteenth century was inevitably going to lead to an increase in poverty, particularly when the amount of land available for cultivation could not be increased and there were few opportunities for jobs in industry. The population rise also put pressure on the limited food supplies, which forced prices up and drove many into destitution. It must also be remembered that as the population was young, there were more consumers than producers, which would also push increasing numbers into poverty.

The price rise and inflation

Inflation meant that many labourers simply found that their wages were not enough to live on. It is estimated that a labourer's wages were worth only half as much at the end of the sixteenth century as they were at the beginning. The situation was particularly bad when there were harvest failures, or even worse, a series of failures, as this drove up the cost of food to very high levels. The Statute of Artificers of 1563, which placed an upper limit on the wages of skilled labourers, may also have had an impact.

Disease and illness

Outbreaks of illness such as influenza, which affected the end of Mary's reign, could have a devastating impact. They could prevent people working, creating temporary poverty, or kill

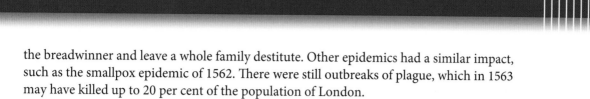

the breadwinner and leave a whole family destitute. Other epidemics had a similar impact, such as the smallpox epidemic of 1562. There were still outbreaks of plague, which in 1563 may have killed up to 20 per cent of the population of London.

Enclosure

Contemporaries frequently blamed enclosure for poverty in the countryside. The switch from arable farming to sheep meant that fewer men were needed, and there were frequent complaints that it resulted in labourers' homes and sometimes whole villages being pulled down and inhabitants evicted. The use of the commons by landowners sometimes resulted in the eviction of squatters, the poorest elements of society who had built their homes on the common land and were now forced to seek work in the towns.

Warfare

The lack of a permanent standing army meant that the Tudors levied soldiers for a campaign and then disbanded them once the war was over. With limited employment opportunities on their return, many turned to begging or theft. Although the navy was on a more permanent footing, it made little provision for those who were injured during campaigns, apart from issuing them with licences to beg.

Harvest failure

Harvest failure created near-famine or famine conditions and forced up prices to a level that many wage labourers were unable to afford. It would have a particular impact in areas that relied on importing corn, particularly urban areas, as they would find it even harder to obtain supplies at a price labourers could afford.

Decline of towns

This is a subject of much debate among historians. However, it is generally agreed that many towns declined in the first half of the sixteenth century. This was for a number of reasons, but all were connected to poverty. Cathedral towns were hit by the dissolution of the monasteries; empty property was often bought up by speculators and then occupied by labourers who had come from the countryside looking for work. As taxes and rates rose, the wealthier citizens moved out. At the same time, many industries moved to the countryside to escape the control of guilds; this was particularly true of the cloth industry. All of this meant that when labourers came to the towns in search of jobs there was little chance of finding work, but the availability of housing encouraged the drift. This brought large numbers of poor people together, which the authorities saw as presenting a considerable danger.

The dissolution of the monasteries (see Chapter 3, pages 62–64)

Some monasteries had been centres of charity and provided care for the sick and poor, and their closure by 1540 removed an element of support from the poorer elements of society. Monasteries were also centres of employment, and their closure left people such as servants without jobs. At the same time, former monks were turned out without the skills to find new jobs. The dissolution also had an impact on the towns where monasteries were located, as the monasteries had brought in visitors, and their decline would have an impact on the trade of the town.

4 What were the effects of social and economic change in the period 1536–69?

ACTIVITY

Read Sources O–R on the causes of poverty, then answer the following question.

Using your own knowledge, assess the interpretation that the most important cause of poverty was idleness.

Sources

O This source describes the impact of the closure of monasteries on northern society.

Many of the said monasteries were in the mountains and deserted places, where the people were in a poor condition and were not taught the law of God, and when the said abbeys stood, the people not only had worldly refreshing of their bodies, but also spiritual refuge. Many of their tenants were fed there and serving men were well looked after by the abbeys; and now … these tenants and servants lack refreshment, both of meat, cloth and wages and do not know if they have any living.

Extract from the Examination of Robert Aske about his role in the Pilgrimage of Grace, 1537 (see Chapter 5, pages 126–130).

P The citizens of London offer their explanation for poverty.

And first may it please your honours to understand, that it was all too evident to all men that beggary and thievery were prominent everywhere. We remembering how many statutes from time to time have been made to redress this, but little change has followed, have sought to find the cause, and after due examination we evidently perceived that the cause of all this misery and beggary was idleness: and the means and remedy to cure the same must be by its contrary, which is labour. And it has been a speech used by all men, to say unto the idle, work! Work! even as though they would have said, the means to reform beggary is to fall to work.

And we considered also that the greatest number of beggars fallen into misery by lewd and evil service, by wars, by sickness, or other adverse fortune, have so utterly lost their credit, that though they would show themselves willing to

labour, yet are so suspected and feared by all men that few will employ them.

A declaration from the citizens of London to the Privy Council, 1552.

Q A contemporary describes the impact of the slump on the cloth trade, 1554.

Infinite numbers of spinners, carders and pickers of wool are turned to begging, with no small store of poor children who, driven with necessity that has no law, both come idly about to beg, to the oppression of the poor husbandmen, and rob their hedges of linen [people used to spread laundry on bushes to dry], steal pigs, geese and capons, steal fruit and corn in the harvest time, and rob barns in the winter time.

R This source outlines some of the causes of poverty in Norwich, the second-largest city in England.

Robert Rowse, 46 years old, glazier, not in work, and Elizabeth, his wife, spins white warp [thread for weaving]; and 5 children, 2 sons, the eldest 16, and the rest daughters who spin and have always lived here.

Agnes Nicols, widow, 40 years old, that sews and has always lived here.

Anne Buck, widow, 46 years old, a teacher of children, two children of nine and five, works lace and has always lived here.

Richard Gugle, 30 years old, glazier who does not work and Dorothy, his wife, she spins white warp, they have a young child and have always lived here. Own their home.

Extract from the Norwich Census of the Poor, 1570.

How did the government deal with the problem of poverty and vagrancy?

Poverty was not an item of great importance for Early Tudor governments, and it was only when the problem reached crisis levels that the government started to intervene. However, as the period progressed the government was forced to take more and more action as the problem grew, so that by the end of the Elizabethan period a whole series of Poor Laws were in place that would last for over 200 years.

At the start of the sixteenth century the poor were usually looked after by the Church, often through generous bequests from wealthy merchants, or by their own families and friends. The Church had provided shelter in almshouses or monasteries, but there were concerns that the dissolution of the monasteries would have an enormous impact on the provision of care for those suffering from poverty. However, it has been shown that monasteries often contributed only 2 or 3 per cent of their income to poor relief, and therefore the dissolution had little impact.

Initially the government was not aware that poverty might be avoidable or that intervention might be needed. Only when it became clear that the poor might be a threat to law and order did they become concerned. As a result, much of the legislation was harsh: punishments for begging were strict and vagrants were returned to their parish of origin so that the problem did not spread. Throughout the period the government drew a distinction between the 'impotent poor' – those who were unable to work because they were old, ill or handicapped – and the 'able-bodied or idle poor' – those who were capable of work, but were lazy. Those who were unable to work needed support, which was to be provided by the community in which they lived. The idle poor were to be either encouraged or forced to work, so that they did not become vagrants and a drain on society. As a result, a series of Acts of Parliament was passed during the sixteenth century (see Table 4.3).

Year	Impotent poor	Idle poor
1531	Allowed to beg in their own parish, but had to obtain a licence. If they begged without a licence they were fined.	Whipped and sent back to parish of origin. Fined for begging without a licence.
1536	Voluntary contributions were given by parishioners to assist in looking after the impotent poor.	Whipped and sent back to parish of origin. Fined for begging without a licence. Children were taken from their parents and put to work.
1547	The Church was to collect money to support the impotent poor, with boxes in churches. Houses were to be built to accommodate the poor.	Those unemployed for more than three days were classed as vagrants. Those convicted of begging were branded and given to the informant as a slave for two years. A second conviction resulted in further branding and slavery for life. A third conviction resulted in the death penalty.

4 What were the effects of social and economic change in the period 1536–69?

1552	A compulsory census and registration was taken. The Church took a more active role in encouraging people to contribute to poor relief.	Whipped and returned to parish of origin. Children were taken from their parents and put to work.
1563	Those who refused to contribute could be taken to court and even imprisoned.	Whipped and returned to parish of origin.
1572	Contributions to poor relief were made compulsory. Overseers of the poor were appointed for each parish; their job was to organise the poor relief.	The first distinction was made between the 'idle poor' and those who were unemployed. Punishments for vagrancy were increased; those seen as deserving poor were excluded from punishment.

Table 4.3   Acts of Parliament passed during the sixteenth century and the measures they recommended for dealing with the poor.

ACTIVITY

1   Using Table 4.3, consider how the government's response to the problem of poverty changed between 1536 and 1569.

2   Which of the statements below best describes government attitudes towards poverty and vagrancy in the period?

  a   The government's main concern was to prevent disorder.

  b   Legislation was largely savage and failed to recognise that many were not idle out of choice.

  c   The government gradually realised that there was a variety of causes of poverty and acted accordingly.

  d   The government gradually realised that they had a responsibility to look after the poor.

Government legislation can be divided into three areas:

1   A campaign against vagrants.

This can be seen in every piece of legislation from the start to the end of the period.

The legislation was savage, with 1547 being the most extreme due to poor harvests and the large number of demobilised soldiers. It was so severe that very few were willing to enforce it, and it was repealed in 1549.

2   The movement to compulsory poor rates.

This started in 1536, with alms to be placed in a 'common box' and by 1563 those who refused to give were to be imprisoned. By 1572 the Poor Rate was made compulsory.

3   Provision of work.

Attempts were made to start this process in 1536. It was left out of the final Act, but finally came in 1576 when governments realised that there was not enough work available.

It is also worth noticing that legislation usually followed years of crisis, see Table 4.4.

Legislation	Occasion
1530s Acts	These followed the great urban poverty of the 1520s and the dissolution of the monasteries.
1547 and 1552	These followed the poor harvests and the fear of unrest after 1549, particularly with a minor on the throne.
1563	There was concern over the security of the succession after Elizabeth's illness.
1572	This followed the Rising of the Northern Earls; the government feared further disorder.

Table 4.4 The laws for dealing with the poor, and what prompted them.

Source

 An extract from a 1531 Act of Parliament dealing with the poor.

Persons being whole and might in body and able to labour were to be tied to the end of a cart, naked and be beaten with whips till his body be bloody by reason of such whipping, and after shall be enjoined upon his oath to return forthwith without delay to the place where he was born, or where he last dwelled and there to put himself to labour like a true man should.

ACTIVITY

Read Source S and answer the questions.

1 Which class of poor is this part of the Act aimed at?

2 Why did the government take such severe action against this group?

3 What was the weakness of the terms of the Act?

A study of the early legislation suggests that the government genuinely believed that there was work available and therefore anyone who was not working was idle. However, as the period progressed there was an increasing awareness that this was not the case and that genuine unemployment was a major problem, particularly in the years when the cloth trade was in a slump. Therefore, although many of the government Acts were savage, particularly in 1547, there was also a growing awareness that money had to be raised to deal with the problem. Parishes were ordered to raise money to care for their own poor.

4 What were the effects of social and economic change in the period 1536–69?

Source

T **An extract from the 1563 Act for the Relief of the Poor. In the same year, the government also introduced the Statute of Artificers, which tied a man to a trade, again showing that the government believed that unemployment led to vagrancy, which in turn brought about social unrest.**

Gently ask and demand of every man and woman what they, out of their charity, will be content to give weekly towards the relief of the poor. Those refusing to contribute are to be brought before the bishop or JPs [Justices of the Peace] who shall have the authority to commit the said obstinate person to prison and assess, tax and limit every obstinate person who refuses, according to their good discretions and what sum the said obstinate person shall pay.

ACTIVITY

Read Source T and answer the questions.

1   Why do you think the government introduced this legislation?

2   What does this tell us about attitudes towards the poor at the time? Why did people have this view?

Local initiatives

indigent

The very needy who lacked even the basic necessities.

Many of the government Acts were motivated by the fear of social unrest, but there was a gradual shift in attitudes among the ruling class. Much government legislation followed local initiatives, which were often the driving force behind schemes to look after the poor. This can be seen particularly in developments regarding a compulsory poor rate in London, Norwich, Colchester and Ipswich.

Source

U **In 1547, London gave up its reliance on voluntary charity and started to raise a compulsory poor rate. The weekly collection in church was not working and therefore a fixed amount was to be levied.**

*For as much as the late order lately devised and taken by the lord mayor and aldermen for the relief, maintenance and funding of the poor, sick and **indigent** persons appointed to be found and kept within the house and lately erected and founded by the most noble prince of famous memory King Henry the eighth the costs and charges to the citizens and inhabitants of this city from the profits and revenues of such lands and tenements as his highness endowed the same house and from charitable alms of the people weekly to be gathered within the parish churches is insufficient. It is therefore for the remedy and support thereof this day by the lord mayor, aldermen and commons in this present common council assembled and authority of the same ordained, enacted, granted and established that the citizens and inhabitants of the said city shall forthwith contribute and pay towards the sustenance, maintaining and funding of the said poor personages.*

Extract from the London Guildhall Journal, 1547, a day-to-day record of events in the City of London.

A similar scheme was introduced in Norwich in 1549 and in Colchester and Ipswich in 1557. Ipswich also established a school for young poor, a local house of correction and a hospital for the poor. Norwich followed with a detailed town plan to deal with poverty and vagrancy in 1570. It was the success of these schemes that encouraged the government legislation of 1563 and 1572.

The growing awareness of the problem was also reflected in the founding of five London 'hospitals' or charitable homes for the poor in the period 1547–53. This was a clear sign of the growing awareness of the different categories of poor, as each hospital was established for a different group.

- St Bartholomew's and St Thomas's were established for the 'impotent poor'.
- Bridewell was used for the 'idle poor'.
- Bedlam was used for those considered to be insane.
- Christ's was for orphans.

Figure 4.2   Christ's Hospital, one of the five hospitals or charitable homes established at the end of Edward's reign for the care of the different categories of poor people. Christ's was for orphans.

4 What were the effects of social and economic change in the period 1536–69?

The establishment of such institutions and the sheer numbers who passed through their doors were clear indications of the scale of the problem and help us to understand why the authorities were so concerned.

It is also worth remembering that the problem of poverty and vagrancy was not confined to England; it was a European phenomenon. This is reflected in the similar legislation introduced in a number of European cities and regions:

1522 Nuremburg (Bavaria, modern southern Germany)

1531 Netherlands

1531–35 Lyon (south-eastern France)

1534 Paris

1540 Brandenburg (modern north-eastern Germany)

How successful was legislation in dealing with the problem?

It is difficult to answer this question by considering only the years up to 1569. We need to look beyond our period of study to achieve a more complete answer.

- There was little or no social unrest as a result of poverty.
- The crisis years of the 1590s, when there was famine and starvation, saw little or no unrest.
- The Poor Laws remained in effect for over 200 years, suggesting that the measures had at least brought some social stability.
- Central government had taken on responsibility for helping the poor.
- It was accepted that the more fortunate had a responsibility to help those less fortunate in society through a compulsory poor rate.

---

sturdy vagabond

These were usually healthy men engaged in begging. They were often drunk and were seen as a threat to law and order.

Sources

(V) *It is now ordained that all officers and ministers of every city, shire, towns and parishes of this realm, at the arrival of such poor creature or* **sturdy vagabond** *shall most charitably receive the same and order the same in manner and form following, that is to say; that all the governors and ministers of every city, shire and town shall not only nurture, find and keep all and every of the same poor people by way of voluntary and charitable alms as shall be thought right by their discretion in such a way as none of them out of necessity shall be forced to wander idly and go openly begging for alms; but also to cause and compel all and every sturdy vagabond and valiant beggars to be kept in continual labour, in such ways that they may by their own labour earn their keep.*

Extract from the 1536 Act for the Punishment of Sturdy Vagabonds and Beggars.

(W) *Any person bringing or causing to be brought the said person so living idly and loiteringly to two of the next Justices of the Peace, who hearing proof of the idle living of the said person shall immediately cause the said loiterer to be marked with a hot iron in the breast the mark of V, and adjudge the said person who is living idly to be the slave of the person who reported him for two years. He shall only give the said slave bread and water or small drink and such refuse of meat as he shall think will encourage the said slave to work by beating, chaining or otherwise in such work or labour, no matter how vile it is.*

Extract from the 1547 Act for the Punishment of Vagabonds and for the Relief of the Poor and Impotent Persons.

Sources

 X A beggar being whipped.

Y *If it happens that any parish has in it more poor and impotent folks who are not able to work than the said parish is able to relieve then they shall grant to as many as they think right a licence to beg, get and receive charitable alms from the inhabitants of the county of the said parish, city and towns so charged. The licence will name the places, towns and parishes to which the poor folks may go. If any of the poor folk so licensed go beyond the limits and beg in other places than are in the licence they will be taken for a beggar and be punished according to the 1541 statute and their licence will be taken from them.*

Extract from An Act for the Relief of the Poor, 1555.

Z Two modern historians explain their views about the punishment of vagrants.

The authorities were more concerned with the danger that begging and vagrancy caused to the maintenance of social order than they were with establishing a complex solution to the problem. Most Tudor legislation therefore recommended strict punishment for begging and required the return of the vagrant to his or her original parish, so that the problem would not spread. There was a distinction drawn between the 'impotent poor' and the 'idle poor', but this was a simplistic analysis of the problem. The initiative to tackle social distress and unemployment came from local authorities, not national government.

Angela Anderson and Tony Imperator (2001) *Tudor England 1485–1603*. Hodder.

ACTIVITY

Study Sources V–Z, then answer the following question.

Using your own knowledge, assess the view that the main concern of Tudor authorities in their treatment of the poor in this period was to punish the idle.

Why did the cloth industry decline by the mid-sixteenth century, and how did the government deal with it?

The woollen cloth industry was responsible for the creation of most of the wealth of England; therefore its decline by the mid-1550s had a significant impact on those who worked in the industry and on the wealth of the nation. The decline resulted in thousands of spinners and weavers being thrown out of work and might even have provided Wyatt with many supporters in his abortive rebellion of 1554 (see pages 138–139).

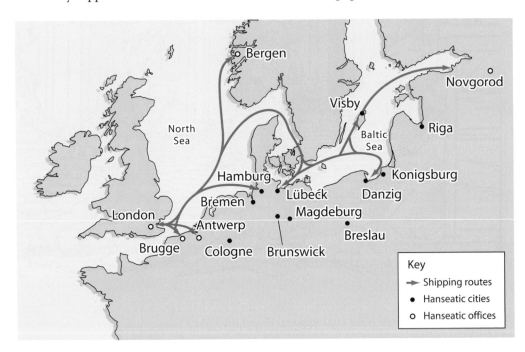

Figure 4.4 The main trading links of London in the mid-sixteenth century.

Although the main cause of this decline was the collapse of the Antwerp cloth market, there were a number of reasons for this, which can be divided into long- and short-term causes.

Long-term causes

- Exports had declined in the fifteenth century, due to a recession in western European trade.
- England was in a weak position diplomatically, as much of the trade was controlled by the **Hanseatic League** and other foreign merchants.
- The English share of trade was dominated by the **Merchant Adventurers**, who had made their base at Antwerp.
- The Antwerp–London trade route meant that English cloth exports were directed from London, which controlled 90 per cent of the exports, to Antwerp, but it also meant that other ports in England declined and that merchants did not look for other markets.

Short-term causes

- There had been a rise in exports in the 1540s due to debasement, which made English goods cheaper, but this meant that when the slump occurred it was even deeper.

Hanseatic League

An organisation of German merchants from ports on the Baltic, who had come together to protect their trade. They dominated the trade of much of northern Europe.

Merchant Adventurers

A group of merchants who, although they traded individually, shipped their cloth together in fleets. Their main centre of trade was Antwerp. They failed to seek other markets, but also stopped other merchants from trading.

- Debasement had also meant that the market for English cloth was saturated and cloth piled up in Antwerp.
- Attempts to deflate the currency in 1551 damaged the credit of English merchants and led to an increase in the price of cloth, although there was some recovery by the end of the 1550s.
- Trade was used as a diplomatic tool, so that when England allied with France in 1550, both England and the emperor placed restrictions on the cloth trade. This was repeated in 1563–64 and 1568–73.
- English merchants had not been willing to look for new markets. It was not until the slump was underway that the **Muscovy Company** was established.
- There was a change in the pattern of demand, as buyers wanted lighter fabrics rather than the heavy English woollen cloth.

Antwerp declined for a variety of reasons:

- The international banking system suffered because of the bankruptcies of French and Spanish monarchs in 1557.
- The outbreak of the **Dutch Revolt** in 1566 led to persecution and hit the city's prosperity.

How did the government try to protect the cloth industry?

Although England was predominantly an agricultural nation, local industry had developed in some areas. The manufacturing of goods, particularly cloth, usually took place in the weavers' cottages, although few worked full time. During the sixteenth century a series of Acts tried to protect the industry as it was such an important employer and generated a considerable amount of revenue.

The government was particularly concerned to protect the quality of the cloth produced, and passed a series of Acts to that end:

1535	Act to maintain standards in making woollen cloth.
1551	Act setting out the standards of cloth and their enforcement.
1551	Act allowing only those who had served proper **apprenticeships** to be weavers.
1554	Act to try to revive the cloth industry and cloth towns by restricting the rules of apprenticeship.
1557	Act restricting cloth manufacture to places where the industry had been established for at least ten years.

> ### ACTIVITY
> How did the government's response to the cloth industry change during the period?

Muscovy Company

With the collapse of the Antwerp market, new sources of trade had to be found. The Muscovy Company was established in 1555 to develop trade with Russia, following the voyages of Sir Hugh Willoughby and Richard Chancellor.

Dutch Revolt

There were many causes of the Dutch Revolt, which broke out in 1562. One was religious division between Catholics and Protestants, which hit Antwerp as the city was blockaded.

apprenticeship

A period of time spent by a student (apprentice) learning his trade from a master craftsman.

E

4 What were the effects of social and economic change in the period 1536–69?

How serious an issue were disease and famine in the period?

After the late 1530s it appears that England did not suffer any serious epidemics of plague until 1550. Both 1551 and 1552 saw outbreaks of sweating sickness (influenza) and plague. In the 1550s, nearly all harvests were below average: there was a run of bad harvests between 1549 and 1551 and again between 1554 and 1556. Those of 1555 and 1556 were particularly bad; they may have caused widespread famine and certainly caused food shortages in the larger towns.

The greatest crisis of the period came towards the end of Mary's reign, with a combination of bad weather and disease. As a result the short-term fluctuations in the grain prices were severe. The poorest harvest of the century so far came in 1556, due to 'the greatest rain and floods that was ever seen in England', which resulted in 'both men and cattle drowned'. The consequences were dire: the price of corn doubled and many were reduced to eating bread made from acorns. This was followed by an epidemic which swept the country between 1556 and 1558 and resulted in a very high mortality rate. Unlike the plague, it was not seasonal, and it hit the countryside as much as the towns. It is uncertain how many died, but estimates have put the figure at 11–20 per cent of the population. This episode clearly illustrates how closely connected the problems of disease and starvation were:

- Those who had been weakened by hunger caused by the harvest failure, were more likely to fall ill.
- The infection spread rapidly as starving people moved in search of food.

Under Elizabeth the country was remarkably free from epidemics. The sweating sickness appears to have disappeared after the 1550s and plague was usually confined to the towns, although there was an outbreak in 1562.

Was there a crisis in the economy and society?

Having read the chapter and studied the sources, you should be able to make your own judgement. It is certainly true that the economic conditions in England during this period did not favour the lower orders of society. Their standard of living had been reduced by the population increase and the price rise, so that many were driven into poverty. This was made worse by the debasement of the currency and the decline in the cloth trade. It is perhaps therefore little wonder that there were large popular disturbances in 1549 (see Chapter 5, pages 144–146). However, the decline in popular unrest in the 1550s suggests that if there was a crisis it was short-lived and that the government had been able not only to contain the problems, but to overcome them.

> ### ACTIVITY
> In order to reach a judgement as to whether there was a crisis in the economy and society, draw up a chart with arguments for and against the view that there was a crisis. Award each argument a mark out of ten, and explain why you have given it the mark, depending on how convincing the argument is. Which argument has the higher total? You have now reached your conclusion.

This chapter will consider four main questions:

■ What were the causes of rebellion and unrest in the period?
■ What was the nature of the rebellion and unrest?
■ How serious a threat was the unrest to Tudor government?
■ How successful were the rebellions?

In terms of skills, there will be opportunities to consider source material and to evaluate series of sources. There will be the chance to review and practise early source-analysis skills, comparison, considering the value and utility of evidence and relating contextual knowledge to sources.

The Exam Café (pages 162–175) will give you the opportunity to consolidate your skills and knowledge by considering answers to real OCR questions at different levels.

Introduction

This chapter will consider the wide range of unrest that threatened Tudor government and society in the period 1536–69. It starts with an analysis of the different causes of the rebellions, looking at the role of politics and faction, religion and social and economic grievances. It will make you aware of different historians' interpretations of the causes and encourage you to formulate your own hypotheses about the pattern of unrest.

It will then look at how the rebels protested and their aims in taking up arms: were they attacking national government or local leaders? This will lead to a consideration of whether the unrest was a serious threat to the government or monarchy, particularly in the light of their aims, numbers and actions. Finally, the chapter will consider whether any rebellion achieved its aims or whether they all ended in failure.

Rebellion was a regular occurrence during this period; each monarch faced at least one major rebellion and the unrest was significant enough to threaten the religious changes of all the monarchs, to bring about the removal of a Protector and, for nine days, the absence of a legitimate monarch. According to one historian, the country came close to anarchy.

What were the causes of unrest in the period 1536–69?

In many instances, historians studying the causes of the unrest are fortunate in that the rebels drew up lists of grievances that were sent or presented to the monarch. This was certainly true of the Pilgrimage of Grace, the Western Rebellion, Kett's Rebellion and the Northern Earls. It might therefore be suggested that these demands reveal the causes of the rebellion. However, some historians would argue that the written demands reflect more the concerns of those who drew up the grievances, rather than the rank and file of the rebellion, and that the rebels' actions provide a better indication of the causes.

Figure 5.1 The locations of the unrest.

The Pilgrimage of Grace, 1536

When studying the Pilgrimage of Grace, it is important to be sure which rebellion you are studying, as it has three distinct parts:

■ The Lincolnshire Rising of October 1536

■ The Pilgrimage of Grace from October to December 1536

■ The Cumberland or Bigod Rising of January 1537

The Lincolnshire Rising was probably the spark for the main outbreak of unrest in Yorkshire and other northern counties, and many of the causes appear to have been similar. In Lincolnshire the rebels' demands were affected by the presence of three government commissions who were overseeing the closure of the smaller monasteries (see Chapter 3, page 62), collecting the 1534 subsidy and examining the condition of the clergy. As a result, the rebels' articles drawn up at Lincoln complained about the closure of the smaller monasteries, the Statute of Uses, taxation, the promotion of men of low birth, such as Thomas Cromwell (see Chapter 2, pages 45–48) and **Richard Rich**, and the appointment of certain bishops whom the rebels believed were heretics.

BIOGRAPHY

Sir Richard Rich

A lawyer and minister under the Tudor monarchs. He worked closely with Thomas Cromwell on the dissolution of the monasteries. He was appointed head of the Court of Augmentations, which managed the income from the sale of monastic lands; this helped to make him very unpopular.

Other developments were taking place in Lincolnshire that may also have prompted the rising. In particular, the **Duke of Suffolk**, an outsider to the region and favourite of Henry VIII, had gained large amounts of land and a key role in local government, which had resulted in the exclusion of many local families from office.

Source

(A) **Read the following comments from the modern historian John Fines about the causes of the Lincolnshire rising.**

*All Lincolnshire people felt there had been too much change and that all of it had interfered in local county affairs. The gentry felt they were being invaded from London, **Hussey** felt there was no chance of continuing, as the Statute of Uses would stop local dynasties and they would be replaced by men from court. Meanwhile, monks and nuns wanted to stop the dissolution now; the clergy wanted to stop the plan to change their churches, stop those who were stealing church goods and stop their jobs being changed. The commons also had feelings about their local church: it was where their ancestors were buried, and now they were being told that prayers for the dead were wrong.*

John Fines (1985) BBC A-Level History series.

BIOGRAPHY

Charles Brandon, Duke of Suffolk

A boyhood friend of Henry VIII, who had been given substantial lands in Lincolnshire. This was unpopular because he was not from the county and had no tradition of landholding in the region, and it appeared to exclude many local gentry from the land market.

BIOGRAPHY

John Hussey

By 1536 Hussey was an elderly man, his authority in the north was in decline and his link with other supporters of Catherine of Aragon did not help his position.

The Pilgrimage of Grace has probably caused more controversy among historians than any other Tudor rebellion. Led by the lawyer **Robert Aske**, it was able to attract support from some 40,000 rebels, who outnumbered Henry's forces by five to one when they met at the River Don. Henry, through trickery, was able to persuade Aske that he would listen to the complaints. Aske then persuaded the rebels to disperse.

The following evidence can be used to suggest that the rising was religious.

1   The number of religious demands made by the rebels; religious demands are at the top of their list of complaints.

2   The timing of the rebellion. It occurred immediately after the closure of some of the smaller monasteries, and commissioners were still closing others.

3   The re-opening of monasteries by rebels in Lancashire.

4   The geography of the rising in Lancashire. The key areas were around the most populous monasteries in the county. These areas, where the rising started, were the last to be quietened.

5   The action of the government after the rising.

6   The symbols of the rising. The rebels marched behind the banner of the five wounds of Christ, they sang the Pilgrim Ballad and even the very name suggests religious motives.

7   The government appeared to be launching an attack on traditional religious practices, with attacks on Holy Days, taxes on baptism, burial and marriage.

8   The rumours of further religious changes: some churches would be closed; jewels and plate would be confiscated.

9   Monasteries were often the places where local people worshipped, so their closure would impact on people's ability to obtain salvation and attend religious services.

BIOGRAPHY

Robert Aske

Aske was probably born around 1500, into an East Yorkshire family of landowning gentry. He was not the eldest son, so did not inherit the land. Instead, he trained as a lawyer in London and became legal advisor to the Earl of Northumberland. His involvement in the rising is difficult to determine, as all the evidence comes from Aske himself. He claimed that he was captured by the Lincolnshire rebels and forced to take their oath. His gradual involvement in the rising is difficult to determine, but at some point it appears he was shown a copy of the rebels' demands and this persuaded him that they agreed with his aims. As a result, he started to gather men and take a more significant role in the rising.

The following evidence can be used to suggest that the rising had either economic or political motives:

Economic

1   There was a bad harvest in 1535, and 1536 was little better.

2   The demands for taxation, particularly the 1534 subsidy.

3   Rumours of new taxes on sheep and cattle, but with livestock numbers low due to bad weather this added to concerns.

4 **Entry fines** were being increased at an alarming rate as landowners tried to make up for the losses caused by inflation.

5 The problems caused by enclosure, though these were regional and limited to the West Riding of Yorkshire and the Lakes.

6 The Statute of Uses, which allowed the heirs of the gentry to avoid paying inheritance tax.

7 The economic function of the monasteries: they played a vital role in the local economy as employers and purchasers; they were crucial in times of hardship; they maintained roads and bridges.

Political and factional

1 The rebellion was the final part of the struggle between the supporters of Catherine of Aragon and the Boleyn faction. Having been defeated both at court and in Parliament, rebellion was the only way for Catherine's supporters to regain influence and to make Henry change his policy.

2 Henry's centralising policy, which was undermining the strong feudal ties in the north of England.

3 The dominance of men of low birth such as Cromwell and Rich.

4 The demand that Mary be restored to the succession.

5 The involvement of people such as Hussey, Aske, **Darcy** and **Constable**, who all had links with Catherine of Aragon and her circle (see Chapter 2, pages 37–38). Some of these had even spoken to the Imperial Ambassador about a rising.

entry fines

Sums of money paid when a tenant farmer died and his son or heir wished to take over the land. In the Pilgrims' demands they are also called 'gressoms'.

BIOGRAPHIES

Thomas, Lord Darcy

A member of a Yorkshire gentry family. Under Henry VII, he had been given a number of military commands for his loyal service, and in 1505 he was made a noble. His position at court declined when Wolsey was in power and deteriorated further with Henry's divorce. He was 67 when the Pilgrimage began. He was custodian at Pontefract Castle when confronted by Aske and joined the Pilgrimage. During his trial, he claimed that he had only joined the rebellion because of threats and was loyal, using his position to lessen the dangers. However, he had discussed the possibility of rebellion with the Imperial Ambassador in 1534 and 1535, and had even drawn up a plan of action.

Sir Robert Constable

Lord of Flamborough and 36 other manors, making him an important local landholder. He, along with Aske, had connections with the Earl of Northumberland.

Source

B An extract from the final set of demands drawn up by the rebels at Pontefract in Yorkshire to present to the King. They set out the overall aims of the campaign.

To have the Pope restored as the supreme Head of the Church.

To have the Lady Mary made legitimate.

To have the abbeys restored to their houses, lands and goods.

To have heretics punished by burning.

To have the Lord Cromwell and Sir Richard Rich punished.

To have a parliament called soon at Nottingham or York.

The Pontefract Articles, December 1536.

ACTIVITY

Read Source B, an extract from the rebels' demands.

In light of the demands, how far do you agree with the interpretation that the Pilgrimage of Grace was mostly caused by religious grievances?

In order to answer this question, you should look at the demands in Source B and see how far they support the view. You should also use the knowledge you have gained from earlier in the chapter and see how far that supports the view.

Discussion point

You need to be clear that there is a difference between the causes of a rebellion and the aims of the rebels.

What do you think were the aims of the rebels? What were they trying to achieve? Do you think that the aims were the same for each group involved? Why and how might they be different?

In the early months of 1537, some of the rebels became convinced that Henry was not going to meet their demands and began another rising. This time the rebels were far fewer and Henry's army was able to crush them at Carlisle. The ringleaders were executed as a warning to other would-be rebels.

The Western Rebellion, 1549

Most historians have seen the Western Rebellion as being predominantly a response to the religious changes of Edward VI (see Chapter 3). This view appears to be confirmed by the rebellion's other name: the Prayer Book rebellion, and the timing of the rising. It started at Sampford Courtenay, in Devon, on the day the First Edwardian Prayer Book was due to be introduced. Even before this there had been religious tensions in Cornwall. William Body, a local archdeacon and Protestant sympathiser, had been attacked in 1547, and was murdered the following year when he returned to the area to supervise the destruction of images on the orders of Protector Somerset, as the government carried out the destruction of many Catholic symbols of worship. This interpretation appears to be confirmed by the

rebels' demands, which were almost exclusively religious. This may not be surprising as they were drawn up by members of the clergy.

Source

 The demands of the Western rebels.

We will have the Six Articles restored.

We will have the sacrament worshipped as it was before, and anyone who disagrees to die like heretics.

We will have images set up and all ancient ceremonies restored.

We will not receive the new service because it is like a Christmas game, but will have our old Latin services. Some of us Cornish men do not understand English.

We will that no gentleman have more than one servant for each hundred marks of land he owns.

We will that half the abbey and chantry lands be taken from their new owners, and two abbeys restored in every county.

ACTIVITY

1   Compare the demands of the Western rebels (Source C) with those of the Pilgrimage of Grace (Source B). How similar were the demands?

2   Why might the demands of the Western Rebellion have stressed the religious grievances? (Think about who wrote them and why.)

Despite the dominance of religious grievances in these demands, an earlier set of demands put a much greater emphasis on social and economic issues. In the earlier grievances, the rebels complained about the new Sheep Tax and Cloth Tax and the problem of enclosure. These complaints are also supported by the comments of contemporaries.

ACTIVITY

Read again the last demand from the Western rebels' grievances (Source C). Although it appears to be religious, calling for former monastic land to be restored to the Church, it can also be seen to have a social element.

1   In what ways does the demand support the view that the rebellion had a social element?

  ■ Now consider the following events that took place during the rebellion:

  ■ The rebels at Bodmin shouted 'Kill the Gentlemen'.

  ■ In Devon, Hellyons, a gentleman who tried to resist the rebels, was murdered.

  ■ The rebels attacked and robbed the gentry at St Michael's Mount.

  ■ They attacked Trematon Castle, plundered it and put the owner in jail.

  ■ Government forces set fire to barns and homes that made up rebel defences in Crediton, Devon.

  ■ In Exeter, the major city of Devon, the town government organised a continuous guard, provided poor relief and firewood, sold food at a low cost or even gave it away to the poorer elements within the city so that they did not hand the town over to rebel forces.

2   How far do the actions of the rebels suggest that the Western Rebellion was not a religiously motivated rising? What do the actions of the rebels suggest was a major cause of unrest in the West Country?

ACTIVITY

Read Sources D–F, contemporary descriptions of the social situation in the West Country at the time of the rebellion.

Using your own knowledge and the sources, how far do you agree with the interpretation that the main cause of the Western Rebellion was social discontent?

Examiner's advice

This is the type of question that you will have to answer in the examination, but then you will have five sources to use instead of three. You need to group the sources according to whether they agree or disagree with the given view and use your own knowledge to test the comments made by the sources. You will also need to consider the provenance of the sources: can you trust them? You will need to think about who wrote them, why they wrote them and when they wrote them. This evaluation carries a large number of marks and the skill needs to be fully developed.

Sources

D **Lord John Russell, the commander of the government force sent to put down the rising, reporting comments made by the rebels after the rising.**

Some poor men were oppressed with extreme and unreasonable compositions, some grieved with unjust exactions by their landlords, some spoiled by one gentleman, some utterly undone and impoverished by another; … and the whole commons universally vested with extremity, wrong and oppression as no slander or reproach was ever heard or reported like unto this, which at the present to the great disfavour and discredit of all gentlemen of the shire is generally spread and bruited in every honest man's mouth.

E **John Hooper, a radical Protestant reformer, commenting on the causes of unrest.**

The people are sorely oppressed by the marvellous tyranny of the nobility.

F **Van der Delft, the ambassador of Charles V, comments on the causes of unrest.**

The nobles had usurped the peasant's rights, leaving no pasture for sheep and cattle and reducing diets to nothing more than bread and water.

BIOGRAPHIES

Lord John Russell

Commander of the royal army sent to crush the Western Rising. On the way he had to deal with other unrest in Oxfordshire, but he had a large force available, containing many German and Italian mercenaries. The slaughter that followed the rebellion was horrific as rebels were hunted down and killed, many without trial.

John Hooper

A Protestant preacher and Bishop of Gloucester, known for his sympathy towards the poor. He was keen to remove all aspects of Catholicism and enforce a radical Protestantism. Such was his desire for radical change that he came into conflict with other Protestants over clerical dress.

Kett's Rebellion, 1549

Kett's Rebellion was the second large-scale rising in 1549. It took place in East Anglia and is named after its leader, Robert Kett. The rising had started with an attack on the enclosures of a local lawyer, John Flowerdew, who had bought the local abbey church and had started to pull it down. Kett was able to gather a force of some 16,000 men who marched towards Norwich and set up camp at Mousehold Heath on the outskirts of the city. The rebels then proceeded to draw up a list of 29 demands.

Source

G Some of the Norfolk rebels' demands, 1549. Kett and other rebel leaders in Norfolk present their demands to the Privy Council.

We pray that no lord of the manor will use the common land.

We pray that ministers that cannot preach God's Word be dismissed, and replaced by others, chosen by parishioners or lord of the town.

We pray that land that is unreasonably rented may be priced as in 1485, and that when lands change hands, the fees are easy to pay.

We pray that every priest shall reside in his parish so his parishioners may be taught God's laws.

*We pray that all **bond men** may be made free, for God made all free with his precious blood.*

Kett's demands, July 1549.

bond men

Men who owed services or payments in return for land that was rented to them. The services might include military or working on the landowner's land. This term originated in the Middle Ages.

ACTIVITY

Read Source G, then answer the following questions.

1   What do the demands suggest were the main causes of Kett's Rebellion?

2   Compare the grievances in Source G with those of the Western Rebels (Source C). In what ways are they similar and in what ways are they different? (Look particularly closely at the religious grievances.)

3   What do the actions of the rebels suggest were the causes? The list below should help you to decide.

  ■ They established a series of camps at centres associated with local government, such as Norwich, Dereham Market and Ipswich.

  ■ From their camp at Mousehold Heath they issued a series of writs and commissions in the same form as the Crown purveyors to some of the rebels to bring in food and drink.

  ■ The camps administered justice.

  ■ A member of the gentry who tried to negotiate with the rebels took food and drink with him, but was still attacked and only just escaped.

  ■ When the rebels seized Norwich they set fire to the homes of the wealthy.

  ■ There was a lack of respect for their social superiors, as shown in Source H.

Source

(H) **An extract from Nicholas Sotherton's *The Commoyson in Norfolk*. A member of the gentry, Sotherton here describes the behaviour of the rebels outside the walls of Norwich.**

They were so shameless and so desperate that the poor vagabond boys, trouserless and bare arsed, came among the thicket of the arrows and gathered them up. When some of the arrows stuck fast in their legs and other parts they most shamefully turned up their bare bottoms against those who did the shooting.

Nicholas Sotherton, *The Commoyson in Norfolk*, 1549.

ACTIVITY

Read Sources H and I and answer the following questions.

1   What does Source I suggest was the main cause of unrest?

2   What evidence is there from the events of the rebellion to support this view?

3   Using Sources H and I, why might Sotherton want to portray the rebels in a bad light?

4   How reliable is Sotherton's account likely to be?

5   How useful to historians studying Kett's Rebellion is Sotherton's account?

Source

(I) **Nicholas Sotherton, a member of the gentry, describes the scene at Mousehold Heath when gentlemen were put on trial.**

They also pushed their weapons into the gentlemen in order to kill some of those brought to them, and they did this with such malice that one Mr Wharton, who was being guarded by a line of men on both sides all the way from the tree [the oak tree under which Kett sat and from which his council of justice operated] to the city, was pricked with their spears and other weapons on purpose to kill him … and moreover, the rest of the gentlemen they imprisoned were bound with chains and locks and they appointed guards to prevent them from escaping.

Stretch and challenge

1   Do the two rebellions of 1549 have anything in common? (Think about the causes and nature of the unrest and the targets of the rebels.)

2   Should the Western Rebellion be seen as just a religious rising?

3   Was Kett's Rebellion about enclosure?

In order to answer these questions, consider carefully Sources C–I on pages 131–135.

The Lady Jane Grey affair, 1553

It can be argued that the rebellion was an attempt by Northumberland to prolong his political power (see Chapter 2, page 32). He had married his son, Guildford Dudley, to Lady Jane Grey and then persuaded Edward to alter the succession so that both Mary and Elizabeth were excluded. As a result, when Edward died the throne passed to Jane, and if she were to become queen, Northumberland would be able to continue to exercise influence as her father-in-law.

Figure 5.2   Lady Jane Grey.

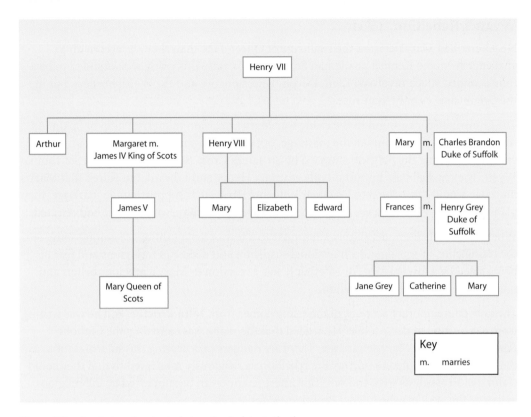

Figure 5.3 Family tree showing Lady Jane Grey's claim to the throne

However, the hand of Edward can also be seen in the planning and execution of the attempt. Edward was a devout Protestant and they have argued that he altered the succession through the devise in order to prevent a Catholic succession. (In order to understand how strong Edward's religious beliefs were, you should refer back to Chapter 3.)

In order to understand the likely motives behind the rebellion, it is necessary to have a firm grasp of the chronology of events. The Succession Act of 1544 had left the crown to Mary and then Elizabeth if Edward died childless. In his will Henry maintained this, but added the descendants of his younger sister, Mary – Lady Frances Grey and her daughters – rather than his elder sister and her descendants.

In the early spring of 1553 Guildford had married Jane, but at this point it was only a good marriage and did not give Northumberland any more power. A few weeks later, Edward signed the devise for the succession, which left the throne to the male heirs of Lady Frances Grey and her daughters. By the end of May 1553, Edward's health was declining fast and he had, at best, two months to live. As a result, the devise was thrown into confusion: there were no male heirs and none would be born before Edward died. It was only then that Edward changed the devise to make Jane queen.

ACTIVITY

Read the chronology of events carefully. What does this suggest about the likely cause of the rebellion? Was it Northumberland trying to preserve his power or Edward trying to preserve Protantism?

Wyatt's Rebellion, 1554

No sooner had Mary defeated the challenge of Queen Jane than she was faced with a challenge from the Kentish gentleman Sir Thomas Wyatt. This rising was intended to be a four-pronged attack involving Kent, Devon, Leicestershire and the Welsh borders, but in the circumstances only Kent rose.

The immediate background to the rising was Mary's decision to marry Philip of Spain. As soon as there were rumours of the marriage, opposition began to surface. It was a conspiracy among the political elites led by Sir James Croft, Sir Peter Carew and Sir Thomas Wyatt. They had all held important offices under Henry and Edward, but feared that Mary's marriage would cause them to lose their influence. Instead of supporting the marriage, they planned to marry the Princess Elizabeth to **Edward Courtenay**, whom Mary had rejected.

Whether this rebellion was simply a response to a fear of loss of influence among some of the ruling elite, or was due to a traditional suspicion and dislike of foreigners and fear of being ruled by a foreign king, or whether it was a reaction to Mary's religious beliefs and policies, needs careful consideration.

The only contemporary account of the rising comes from **John Proctor**, and he was writing from a government perspective. He argued that the rising was caused by the Catholic restoration and not Mary's marriage. There are dangers in accepting this interpretation, as the government wanted to portray the rebellion as religiously motivated so that they could claim that Protestants were traitors. This interpretation can be supported by the religious beliefs of the leaders, who all had Protestant sympathies.

BIOGRAPHIES

John Proctor

The author of *The History of Wyatt's Rebellion*, which was commissioned by the government immediately after the rebellion. This account stresses the importance of religious factors, as the government wanted to divert attention from the unpopularity of Mary's marriage. This means that his account must be treated with caution.

Edward Courtenay

Courtenay was descended from earlier English kings. Gardiner had proposed that Mary Tudor should marry him, as his ancestry would help to strengthen her regime. However, after Mary rejected the plan, a plan for a marriage between Courtenay and Elizabeth was taken up by the leaders of Wyatt's Rebellion.

Source

(J) **In trying to rally support for the rising, Wyatt issued the following proclamation on 25 January. Wyatt was a member of a Kentish gentry family, a committed Protestant who had done well under Edward's rule, particularly after crushing a rising in Kent in 1549.**

We write to you as friends, neighbours and Englishmen, concerning Queen Mary's declared intention to marry a foreigner, and request you to join us to prevent this. We swear to you before God that we seek no harm to the Queen, but merely wish her better advice. Our wealth and health depend on it. A hundred armed Spaniards have already arrived at Dover and travelled through Kent on their way to London. We require you to assemble with as much support as possible, to help us protect liberty and the commonwealth.

ACTIVITY

Read Source J, then answer the following questions.

1   What does Wyatt's proclamation suggest was the cause of the rising?

2   How does he try to attract support for the rising? What does he claim? Why would this attract supporters?

3   How far does Wyatt's proclamation disagree with the view put forward by John Proctor in Source O on page 141? Why does Wyatt's proclamation not stress religion as a cause? (It might help to re-read Chapter 3.)

It should be remembered that it was almost impossible to separate politics and religion at this time. Mary's marriage to Philip also had a religious element, as it would strengthen England's links to the major European Catholic power and, if a child was born, would secure a Catholic succession. At the same time it should also be noted that the area around Maidstone, the centre of the rising, had just seen a decline in the cloth trade and rising unemployment. However, even if economic hardship was the motive for some, others were involved for factional reasons. Mary's accession had seen a shake-up in office-holding in local government and many had lost positions of influence, particularly after the Lady Jane Grey affair. They would feel that with the arrival of Spaniards their chances of ever regaining their influence were even further reduced.

We might therefore suggest that the rebels' motives varied considerably and that their involvement was simply because there was no other way of protesting.

The Rising of the Northern Earls, 1569

The early years of Elizabeth's reign saw a period of political unity. Cecil worked closely with Elizabeth, but this relationship caused disquiet. A growing number of disgruntled nobles at court, most notably the **Sussex** and Leicester factions, were fed up with the domination of William Cecil (see Chapter 2, pages 56–58). They drew up a plan for Mary Queen of Scots, who had recently fled to England, to marry the Duke of Norfolk. They believed that this would force Elizabeth to name Mary as her heir and would force Cecil out. The scheme was supported by the Earls of Northumberland and Westmorland, both of whom were Catholics. The plan failed and Norfolk was sent to the Tower. At the same time, the northern counties, traditionally conservative in religion, had been subjected to a vigorous

campaign of Protestantism by the new Bishop of Durham. The two earls had also suffered a loss of status under the Elizabethan regime and with the failure of the marriage plan had little chance of regaining their positions. They were not the only northern nobles who felt alienated, as the Queen had brought in her own men, such as Hunsdon, to administer the area.

> **BIOGRAPHY**
>
> **Thomas Radcliffe**
>
> A soldier and administrator who joined the Privy Council in 1565. His religious outlook was neutral and he usually supported Cecil, but in this case he joined with Leicester, showing the fluid nature of factional politics.

> **Source**
>
> **K** An extract from the Proclamation of the Earls, issued at Darlington on 16 November 1569. Similar proclamations were issued at Staindrop and Richmond to rally the north.
>
> *The Earls of Northumberland and Westmorland, the Queen's most true and lawful subjects, send greeting to all her Catholic subjects. Various newly created noblemen have displaced the ancient nobility of this realm from the Queen's side. Over the last twelve years they have maintained a new heretical religion, contrary to God's word. To rectify this, various foreign powers aim shortly to invade England and destroy us, if we do not quickly prevent them. So we have decided to act ourselves, to avoid being enslaved by them.*

> **ACTIVITY**
>
> Read Source K and answer the questions below.
>
> 1   According to the Earls' proclamation, what was the cause of the rising?
>
> 2   How reliable is the proclamation as evidence for the causes of the rising? (Think about its origin and purpose, then look back at the events of 1568–69 – do they support the view put forward by the Earls?)
>
> 3   How far do the actions of the rebels support the view put forward in the proclamation about the causes of the Rising of the Northern Earls (Source P on page 141)?

What did the rebels do?

- They seized Durham Cathedral.
- They carried a banner showing the Five Wounds of Christ.
- They destroyed English Bibles, set up stone altars and reinstated Latin mass.
- The Protestant service book was destroyed in about 70 churches in Yorkshire and eight in Durham.
- Mass was restored in six Yorkshire and eight Durham churches.

These actions prompted the Royal Commander to comment: 'The ancient faith still lay like lees at the bottom of men's hearts and if the vessel was stirred a little came to the top.'

Sources

L **Extracts from the Pontefract Articles, drawn up by the Pilgrims, 1536.**

To have the supreme head of the Church reserved unto the See of Rome as before it was accustomed to be.

To have the suppressed abbeys restored to their houses, lands and goods.

That the lands in Westmorland, Cumberland, Kendall, Dent, Sedburgh, Fornes and the abbey lands in Mashamshire, Kirbyshire, Notherdale may be tenant right, and the lord to have at every change 2 years rent as the entry fine and no more.

To have the statute for enclosure put into execution and all enclosures since the fourth year of Henry VII's reign pulled down except mountains, forests and parks.

To have the Statute of Uses that no man may will his lands to be repealed.

M **A letter to the Senate of Venice, 20 July 1549, from Matteo Dandolo, the Venetian ambassador in England.**

There is news of major risings against the government in England, and that the King has retreated to a strong castle outside London. The cause of this is the common land, as the great landowners occupy the pastures of the poor people. The rebels also require the return of the mass, together with the religion as it stood on the death of Henry VIII. The government, wishing to apply a remedy, put upwards of 500 persons to the sword, sparing neither women nor children.

N **A copy of a letter containing certain news and the requests of the Devonshire and Cornish rebels. Written by a gentleman of Devon, probably to William Cecil, 1549. (At this time, Cecil was Secretary of State to Somerset and a member of his household.)**

I do now include their Articles. I could not well do this before because they changed them so often and devised so many. There were such diversities of heads amongst them that for every kind of brain there was one manner of Article.

The priests all harped upon a plain song of Rome; certain traitors wanted to welcome home Cardinal Pole; a number of vagabonds would have no justice; a band of thieves would have no State of any Gentlemen.

O **From *A History of Wyatt's Rebellion* by John Proctor, 1554.**

Wyatt, proceeding in his detestable purpose, armed himself and as many as he could. And, considering that the restoring of the newly-forged religion was not a cause general enough to attract all sorts to support him, he determined to speak no word of religion but to make the colour of his commotion only to withstand strangers and to advance liberty.

P **From the Proclamation of the Northern Earls, 1569.**

Whereas various newly set up nobles about the Queen's Majesty, have and do daily not only go about to overthrow and put down the ancient nobility of this realm, but also have misused the Queen Majesty's own person, and also have by the space of twelve years past, set up, and maintained a newfound religion and heresy, contrary to God's word. For the amending and redressing thereof, diverse foreign powers do purpose shortly to invade this realm, which will be to our utter destruction, if we do not ourselves speedily forfend the same.

Rebellion	Main cause	Supporting evidence	Other causes	Supporting evidence	What was the impact of royal authority?
Pilgrimage of Grace					
Western Rebellion					
Kett's Rebellion					
Lady Jane Grey affair					
Wyatt's Rebellion					
Rebellion of the Northern Earls					

What was the nature of the challenge to royal authority?

There is much debate about the social groups who led the rebellions during this period. This has largely centred on the role of the gentry who, it might be argued, were the ringleaders. However, it can be argued that many of the risings had more popular origins and that the gentry were only involved because they were either coerced or persuaded to act as leaders. Given the hierarchical nature of Tudor society, it should perhaps come as no surprise that the commons often looked to the gentry to lead the risings as they could provide organisation and perhaps give the unrest some sort of legitimacy.

Whatever the reasons for the gentry's involvement, it did make a rising a greater challenge to royal authority as the very members of society who should have been keeping order in the localities were actually undermining stability and threatening order.

The Lincolnshire Rising and the Pilgrimage of Grace, 1536

This rising perhaps caused most controversy in the period. Not only have its causes been hotly debated, but also its nature. Was it a spontaneous rising of the commons or an attempted court factional coup led by gentry who felt excluded?

The Lincolnshire rising was led by gentry, but were they coerced and threatened with the loss of their goods, or even their lives, if they did not take part?

Source

Ⓠ **An extract from notes taken during the interrogation of Nicholas Leche, a priest involved in the rising. Leche was taken to the Tower, where he was interrogated. These notes are a record of the interrogation.**

He thinks all the exterior acts of the gentlemen along with the commons were done willingly, for he saw them as willing to set forward their views in the same way as the commons were. And further, during the whole time of the insurrection, not one of the gentlemen persuaded the people to stop or showed them it was high treason ... The gentlemen were the first armed of all the people, and commanded the commons to prepare themselves.

ACTIVITY

Read Source Q and answer the questions below.

1 Who does Leche blame for the unrest?

2 Why might he blame them? What is his purpose?

3 How reliable is Leche's confession as evidence for the nature of the unrest? (You need to think about the purpose of his confession and compare what he says with the complaints of the rebels.)

Some gentry claimed that their aim was to gain control of the rising, while others argued that they became involved in order to stop the commons from becoming too aggressive.

The clergy and monks also played a significant role. They supported the rebels with money and there is also evidence that the parish clergy helped to mobilise the movement. There are even stories of armed monks joining. However, although the parish clergy played an important role, the leaders of society in the villages and small towns, the richer yeomen and substantial tradesmen, who often acted as churchwardens and parish constables, were more important. Their roles in local government had given them the experience in leadership and respect in local society that were necessary to lead a rebellion.

The main element of the Pilgrimage of Grace has caused even greater controversy. It was led by Robert Aske, a lawyer whose work brought him into contact with people at court and with all elements of society, which may have made him the ideal rebel leader. He claimed he was a reluctant leader, having been stopped by a group of men who demanded that he take an oath of loyalty to their cause when they found out that he was a gentleman. He was shown a copy of the rebels' demands and felt that they fitted his ideas, and so he began to muster men. This raises the question of why he decided to throw in his lot with the rebels and take on a prominent role. It might be argued that the rising was the response of a defeated court faction who were determined to create a power base in the country from which to launch another assault to restore their fortunes at court. This suggests that the rising was not spontaneous, but was planned by members of the court, such as Darcy and Hussey, who had been supporters of the late Queen Catherine. There is significant debate about Darcy's role, however: some have claimed that his plans for a rising were no more than empty boasting, while others have claimed that he had been discussing the idea of rebellion with the Imperial Ambassador since 1534.

Source

R Darcy himself claimed that he joined the rebellion under duress and that he attempted to use his position to minimise the effects:

I would choose death of body before life rather than your Majesty think that I should by freewill unforced and sore compelled by the extreme compulsion and fury of the commons enter into their companies and great follies.

From a letter by Lord Darcy to Henry VIII, January 1537.

ACTIVITY

Using the sources and the information in the text, who do you consider to be the persons mainly responsible for the rising?

However, it can be argued that the Pilgrimage was primarily a rising of the commons. All nine of the rebels' host armies began as a protest of the people, but their belief in hierarchy or a 'society of orders' led them to demand that the local gentry or noble families take the leadership. This interpretation can be supported by the original title of the rising, which was a 'pilgrimage for grace for the commonwealth', which meant the ordinary people. This, it can be argued, was reflected in their complaints about heavy taxation, the attacks on tenant rights and on the wealth of their local churches.

The Western Rebellion, 1549

An examination of the rebels' actions (see activity on page 132) suggests that this rebellion was primarily a rising of the commons and even Article 13, which called for a limit to the number of servants that a gentleman could have, supports this view. This is made even clearer in the reply (Source S) given to the rebels by Thomas Cranmer (see Chapter 2, pages 48–50).

Sources

S From Cranmer's reply to the rebels:

Was it ever seen in any country since the world began, that the commons did appoint the nobles and gentlemen the number of their servants? Standeth it with any reason to turn upside down the good order of the whole world that is the commoners are to be governed by the nobles and the servants by their masters? God will not allow this, but will take vengeance of all who break his order.

T An extract from a letter by William Paget to Protector Somerset on 7 July 1549, warning him of the dangers of his policy.

The foot taketh upon him the part of the head, and commons is become a king, appointing conditions and laws to the governors, saying, 'Grant this, and that, and we will go home.'

ACTIVITY

Compare the responses of Cranmer and Paget (Sources S and T) as evidence for the nature of the unrest in the West Country in 1549.

The involvement of Humphrey Arundell, a gentleman who owned significant lands around Bodmin, in Cornwall, suggests that it was not just a peasant rising, but he is the only example of gentry involvement. He claimed that he was forced to join the rising, but there is little evidence to support this.

The treatment of Robert Welsh, the vicar of the church of St Thomas, might suggest that the clergy led the rebellion, and this view is supported by the nature of the rebels' demands, which focused heavily on religious grievances. At the end of the rising, Welsh was hanged on gallows erected on his church tower, wearing his vestments and with a ' holy-water bucket, a sprinkle, a sacring bell, a pair of beeds and such other like popish trash hanged about him.'

Kett's Rebellion, 1549

There appears little doubt that Kett's Rebellion was primarily a rising of the commons. Kett himself was a well-to-do tanner and came from that element of society just below those involved in local government. He owned a significant amount of land in the area and was also a prominent member of the local church.

> **Currency in England**
>
> s = shilling, there were 20 of these in £1.

Sources

(U) **An extract from the Accounts of Robert Raynbald, Chamberlain of the City of Norwich, writing in 1550 after Kett's Rebellion. His account shows that Kett's support came from those of a similar social standing as Kett, or lower.**

City Butchers

*Item of Thomas Toly for the first half year farm [rent] of the 4th and 5th stalls both in one: **8s***

And of him for the last half year: nothing, forasmuch as he was hanged as a traitor.

*Item of Edmond Fereby for the first half year farm of the 10th stall: **10s***

And for the last half year nothing was, forasmuch as the said Fereby was a rebel in Mousehold who fled and left nothing which could be seized.

(V) **Nicholas Sotherton, a member of the gentry, describes the behaviour of the rebels outside the city walls of Norwich.**

They were so shameless and so desperate that the poor vagabond boys, trouserless and bare arsed, came among the thicket of arrows and gathered them up. When some of the arrows stuck fast in their legs and other parts they most shamelessly turned up their bare bottoms against those who did the shooting.

Sotherton also claims that:

Various of the best citizens of Norwich, with their wives and children were quick to depart the city as they would not obey the rebels.

(W) **Protector Somerset writes to a close advisor expressing his view of the rebels. This was written on 24 August 1549.**

Some rebels wish to pull down enclosures and parks; some want to recover their common land; others pretend religion is their motive. A number would want to rule for a time, and do as gentlemen have done, and indeed all have a great hatred of gentlemen and regard them as their enemies. The ruffians among them, as the soldiers, who are leaders, look for loot. So the rebellions are nothing other than a plague and a fury among the vilest and worst sort of men.

ACTIVITY

Using Sources U–W and your own knowledge, assess the interpretation that Kett's rebels came from the lower elements in society.

The rebels themselves were socially conservative in their outlook. They believed that they had the support of the government and saw themselves as the guardians of tradition and custom. They saw their grievances as legitimate and felt that protest was the best way to bring their problems to the attention of the government. This outlook is reflected in the construction of their demands, as each article began with the phrase 'We pray …'. This is hardly the language of revolutionaries looking to overturn society.

ACTIVITY

1 Compare the language and tone used by the rebels in Kett's Rebellion with that used in the Pilgrimage of Grace (Source B page 130) and the Western Rebellion (Source C page 131).

2 What does this tell us about way the rebels saw themselves?

3 Why might they want to be seen in this way?

Wyatt's Rebellion, 1554

The initial conspiracy had been formed by a group of gentry. The leading conspirators were William Thomas, a former clerk of the Council to Edward VI; Sir James Croft, Lord Deputy of Ireland in 1551–52 and Sir Peter Carew, who had acted for Somerset against the western rebels in 1549 and had sat in Edward VI's Parliament as knight of the shire for Devon in 1553. The final conspirator was Sir Thomas Wyatt, a gentleman who had been brought up as a Catholic; he had been sent to court at a young age and later fought loyally for the Crown under both Henry VIII and Edward VI. The shock of seeing the Spanish Inquisition at work may have made him hostile to Spaniards. This, and the fear that the arrival of Spaniards, following Mary's plan to marry Philip, would block any chance of promotion at court, may have pushed him into rebellion.

There were many disincentives for gentry to become involved in rebellion. Their social position depended on social stability and they were frequent recipients of patronage from the Crown, who often saw them as counterweights to powerful nobles. Lastly, they also feared unrest among the lower orders and had often been involved in crushing unrest in 1549.

ACTIVITY

Why might members of the gentry become involved in rebellion?

The Northern Earls, 1569

The leadership of this rebellion was undoubtedly aristocratic. The Earls of Northumberland and Westmorland were the key nobles in the northern counties of England and had become frustrated at being sidelined by Elizabeth and her government, which had an impact both on their status and their financial situation. At the same time, they were angered by the development of a more Protestant Church in the north of England, following the appointment of a new bishop of Durham. Northumberland had suffered severely from Elizabeth's reassertion of the policies of her father, aimed at weakening the hold of the great magnate families on the Marches.

BIOGRAPHIES

Thomas Percy, 7th Earl of Northumberland

A member of the traditional leading noble family of the area, which was losing influence as Elizabeth built up the status and influence of his major rival, Sir John Forster. Having been restored to his position by Mary Tudor, Northumberland was losing influence in controlling the border lands with Scotland, known as the Marches.

Earl of Westmorland

Like Northumberland, a key landowner in the north. He disliked the imposition of a more Protestant Church. He was also suffering a decline in wealth and status, and was so poor that he had been obliged to borrow money.

Figure 5.4   Thomas Percy, 7th Earl of Northumberland.

Sources

Read the following extracts about the background of those involved in the rebellion.

X *Sir John Foster wrote on 24 November that he had just heard that 'the Earls have offered wages of sixteen pence a day to all that will come.' Many undoubtedly joined the rebellion because they feared for their lives and goods. On 17 November Bowes reported to Cecil: 'they have constrained, by force, various of them to follow them; as the people of Bishopton ... they not only forced them to go with them, but compelled the rest of the town, armed and unarmed, to go to Draneton.'*

The strength of the rebel army lay in their horsemen, who were gentlemen, and their household servants and tenants.

A. Fletcher (2004) *Tudor Rebellions*. Longman.

Y *The rebellion was strikingly non-feudal: nine-tenths of the known rebels were not tenants of the leaders and there was much more of a popular movement than has been supposed.*

C. Haigh (1988) *Elizabeth I*. Longman.

Stretch and challenge

1 What do Sources X and Y suggest were the reason why people joined the rebellion?

2 Using the sources and your knowledge from the chapter, how far do you agree with the interpretation that the rising was primarily an aristocratic uprising?

(Note that you will not be asked to compare secondary sources in the exam, however this activity will help you prepare for the coursework element of A2.)

ACTIVITY

Complete a copy of the table below, which will help you summarise the leadership of the rebellions.

Leadership	Pilgrimage of Grace	Western Rebellion	Kett's Rebellion	Wyatt's Rebellion	Rebellion of the Northern Earls
Nobility					
Gentry					
Yeomanry					
Commons					
Clergy					

In light of the table above, formulate your own hypothesis about the leadership of rebellions in the period. Think carefully about whether leadership remains the same or changes. If it changes, when does this happen and why?

What does the changing nature of the leadership of the rebellions suggest about the changing nature of the challenge to royal authority?

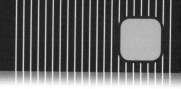

What was the nature of the challenge to royal authority?

In considering the challenges to royal authority it might be a good idea to start by establishing a series of criteria that make the challenge serious.

1   Number of rebels. A large number of rebels would make a rising more challenging, as the government lacked a standing army and relied on local nobles and gentry raising forces or on bringing in mercenaries to disperse the rebellion. This meant that the government always tried to negotiate with the rebels and persuade them to disperse.

2   Nature of the rebellion. A rebellion led by either the nobility or gentry was likely to be better organised and to have a greater sense of legitimacy. It would become an even greater challenge if it was able to attract support from all classes of society.

3   Location. The location of a rebellion is an interesting point of debate. Was a rebellion more challenging if it was a long way from London because it would take the government a long time to send forces and therefore give the rebellion a chance to develop, or was it more serious near London because it could be a direct threat to the government?

4   Aims. A rebellion that aimed to remove the monarch was a greater challenge than one that was protesting about government policy, such as religious or economic changes.

5   Timing. A number of rebellions happening simultaneously would be much harder for the government to deal with, as their forces would be divided. Likewise, a rebellion could be more dangerous if it occurred at the start of a monarch's reign, or at the same time as a threat of foreign invasion, or when a minor was on the throne.

6   Actions of the rebels. Rebellions that march on London or take major cities might be considered to be more serious than those that establish camps and do not move.

In light of the above, Table 5.1 offers a summary of the challenge presented by each rebellion.

Rebellion	Argument that it was a serious challenge	Argument that it was not a serious challenge
Pilgrimage of Grace	The rebels numbered over 40,000 and outnumbered royal forces 5:1.	They did not aim to overthrow Henry, just his ministers.
	They held Pontefract Castle, a key to the north.	It was aimed at reversing policy, not changing the dynasty.
	They took York, the major city of northern England.	The rebels did not march south.
	It was a cross-class rebellion, involving nobility, gentry and the commons.	The rebel leadership was willing to negotiate.
	Henry was willing to negotiate.	
Western Rebellion	It took five battles or skirmishes to put it down.	The grievances were religious and economic; they were not aimed at removing the King.
	The timing coincided with unrest in other areas so resources were stretched.	

	It coincided with an invasion from France.	The rebels were unable to take Exeter.
	The monarch, Edward VI, was a minor.	The rebels remained in the West Country and made no attempt to march on London.
	The demands were aggressive: 'we will have'.	It lacked cross-class support. There was noticeable and significant lack of gentry and aristocratic leadership.
	Over 3000 were killed; the government carried out executions without trials.	Virtually no attempt to co-operate with other risings.
	The local gentry failed to deal with the rising. The fall of the Courtenays meant that there were no nobility to deal with the rising.	
	Russell had to raise troops from distant counties as the government dared not risk the loyalty of local peasants.	
	Somerset had to bring troops back from Scotland.	
Kett's Rebellion	Rebels took Norwich, England's second city.	The grievances were largely social and economic, not aimed at central government.
	The timing coincided with unrest in other areas, so resources were stretched.	The demands were presented in a moderate fashion: 'we pray'.
	It coincided with an invasion from France.	The rebels remained camped in East Anglia and made no attempt to march on London.
	The monarch, Edward VI, was a minor.	Kett's leadership was poor. There was an absence of aristocratic and gentry leadership.
	The Earl of Northampton was defeated by the rebels and John Dudley had to be sent.	
	Numbers were large: 16,000.	
	The government slaughtered over 3000 rebels.	
	The local gentry failed to deal with the rising. The fall of the Howards meant that there were no nobility in the region.	
	Somerset had to bring troops back from Scotland.	

Lady Jane Grey rising	Northumberland and his supporters succeeded in placing Jane on the throne for 14 days. Initially it had the support of the Council. They had control of the Tower and the fleet.	Mary escaped and was able to raise forces in East Anglia. There was popular support for Mary. Mary behaved as a queen. It was poorly planned; they failed to arrest Mary. Mary was seen as the legitimate ruler.
Wyatt's Rebellion	The aim was to replace Mary as Queen. The rebels reached London. Troops sent under Norfolk deserted to Wyatt.	It had gentry support only in Kent. Mary remained resolute in London. The rebels were slow in marching on London. The aims of the rebels were unclear. Mary's religious policies were still unclear; burnings had not started. The four-pronged attack did not happen. The timing was poor, it was winter.
The Rebellion of the Northern Earls	Mary Queen of Scots was an alternative ruler and the legitimate queen in the eyes of many Catholics. Elizabeth's reaction once it was over was to execute over 450 people.	Support for the Earls was limited, only 5000. Elizabeth's government in the north was more secure than that of Henry VIII in 1536. The Earls soon turned back when they heard of a large force being sent. Mary Queen of Scots had been moved further south; therefore the rebels were unable to free her. Lack of foreign support, the Pope did not issue the papal bull until after the rising. The rebellion was poorly planned, support was limited geographically and Northumberland lacked the time to mobilise all his tenants. The Earls were unable to get Catholic support in Lancashire and Cheshire. Government officials held key towns.

Table 5.1   The challenges posed by each of the rebellions.

ACTIVITY

In the light of Table 5.1 and your own knowledge, rank the rebellions in order of the challenge they presented to Tudor governments.

Source

Z Historians have disagreed about the threat that rebellion presented to Tudor governments; this is most noticeable in their consideration of events of 1549.

The bulk of the stirs tended to embarrass the government by seeking to implement rather than resist its policy. The government at no point fought for its life. No rising in 1549 threatened the government physically in the manner of those of 1381, 1450 and 1497 with a sustained march on London. Nor did the rebels plan to release the king from the grip of evil ministers. If anything, the aim was to aid the government against the aristocracy, or to make it change its religious policy. Also to the government relief, the 1549 risings stand out for their lack of aristocratic participation and leadership.

M.L. Bush (1975) *The Government Policy of Protector Somerset*. McGill-Queens University Press.

AA *In 1548 the situation had been contained without too much difficulty, which may have induced a sense of false security, but as the summer of 1549 advanced, it looked as though the whole of southern England was on the point of social and economic disintegration. By July the foreign mercenaries, recruited for the war in Scotland, were being deployed against English rebels; and London was garrisoned and protected with artillery.*

C.Loades, *Mid-Tudor Crisis, 1545–1565*. Palgrave Macmillan.

Stretch and challenge

Read Source Z and answer the following questions.

1   What is Bush's view about the seriousness of the risings of 1549?

2   What is his evidence to support his view?

3   Explain the reference to events of 1381, 1450 and 1497.

4   Explain the reference to 'aid the government against the aristocracy.

Read Source AA and answer the questions below.

1   What is Loades' view about the seriousness of the risings of 1549?

2   What is his evidence to support his view?

3   What had happened in 1548 to create a sense of false security?

4   Read Sources Z and AA and study Table 5.1.

Using your own knowledge and the primary sources, which interpretation do you find more convincing. Why?

Note that you will not be asked to compare secondary sources in the exam, but this is good preparation for the A2 coursework.

Sources

BB A letter from the Imperial Ambassador to Charles V, October 1536. He describes events in Lincolnshire and the response of the government. The ambassador himself had been encouraging unrest and had promised the rebels help from Charles.

Five days ago in Lincolnshire a great multitude of people rose against the King's commissioners, who levied the taxes lately imposed by parliament and put down the abbeys. It is said some of the commissioners have been killed. Others, who allowed themselves to be taken, have been compelled to swear fidelity first to God, secondly to the Church and thirdly to the King. The rebel numbers are reckoned by some at 10,000. To judge by the preparations made against them the numbers must be very great and increasing, for there is not a gentleman of influence whom the King has not ordered to be ready with forces. The Duke of Norfolk has left in great haste for Norfolk, both to raise men and to give orders to prevent disturbances there.

CC John Flotman, a captain in Kett's army in 1549, answers charges of treason made against him after the rebellion.

Flotman cared not a pin's point for my lord marquess [Northampton] and, like a rebellious traitor, maintained that he and the rest of the rebels were earnest defenders of the king's royal majesty and that they had taken weapon in hand not against the king, but in his defence. In time it should appear they sought nothing but to maintain his majesty's royal estate, the liberty of their country and the safety of their commonwealth. He utterly refused the king's pardon.

DD In about 1550 the 13-year old Edward VI began to keep a journal of major political events. Here he writes of the troubles of 1549.

The people rebelled in Sussex, Hampshire and Kent, where by fair persuasions, partly from honest men among the rebels, *and partly by local governors, they were satisfied and went home.*

After that, the people rose in Oxfordshire, the West Country and Norfolk. The Marquis of Northampton was sent to Norwich, with 1060 horsemen, but lost 100 men in battle and retreated. The Earl of Warwick replaced him, with 7500 men, and fought the rebels for three days in Norwich before overcoming them outside the city, killing 2000 of them. Then the Council gathered in London, to charge Protector Somerset with allowing these rebellions to occur.

EE Charles Wriothesley, a well-informed contemporary, outlines the major events of Wyatt's Rebellion.

On 29 January the Duke of Norfolk tried to attack Rochester Castle, where the traitor Wyatt and his rebels lay, but he was forced to flee and the rebels captured his artillery. On 1 February Queen Mary went to the city of London, and denounced Wyatt's attempt to take her crown and sack the city. On 3 February Wyatt's army reached London Bridge. On 7 February the Earl of Pembroke gathered the royal army at Charing Cross near the city, but Wyatt and some rebels avoided them and got close to the city, where they were captured.

Charles Wriothesley's *Chronicle of England* for 1554.

FF A modern historian comments on the threat posed by the Rebellion of the Northern Earls.

Elizabeth had blundered: she forced the Earls to choose between flight and rebellion, when rebellion was still a realistic option. They chose rebellion, because of the Catholic enthusiasm of their followers and the scorn of the Countess of Westmorland ... so the Earls rebelled, more in sorrow than in anger: men who had been planning rebellion for weeks, even months, were forced into an unplanned rising. But it was still a dangerous rising, which could use powerful slogans. The revolt was presented in traditional terms as the revenge of the old nobility against upstart evil counsellors.

C. Haigh (1988) *Elizabeth I*. Longman.

ACTIVITY

Read Sources BB–FF about the seriousness of unrest in the period from 1536 to 1569. Using the sources and your own knowledge, how far do you agree with the interpretation that Wyatt's Rebellion was the most serious challenge to Tudor government?

Figure 5.5 Queen Elizabeth I, painted c. 1558.

What was the impact of the rebellions on royal authority?

On the surface, it appears as if rebellion had little impact. All the rebellions in this period appear to have failed and many of the rebels were killed. Yet if rebellions constantly failed, why did people continue to rise in rebellion? Although the rebels' stated aims may not have been achieved, other issues were often resolved, or sometimes other concerns that were not mentioned in the demands were addressed. It is also likely that many of those who took part in the rebellions had different aims and grievances from those outlined in the written demands, and this makes it even more difficult to judge how far the rebels achieved their aims. Different groups within a rebellion would have wanted different things, making the task harder for the historian. It should also be remembered that for many, rebellion was the only way to let the government know of their dissatisfaction. In these instances, simply raising a rebellion and drawing the attention of government to the problem was success in itself. It is also difficult to know whether government action and reform after a rebellion that appears to deal with rebel grievances were the direct result of the rebellion or were part of general policy that would have happened anyway.

On the surface, the Pilgrimage of Grace failed in its aim of reversing the religious changes that Henry was undertaking. It might even be argued that the rebellion hastened the closure of the larger monasteries, as Henry saw all monasteries as centres of resistance. The rising in early 1537 also gave Henry the opportunity to go back on the promises he had made to Aske, and it resulted in the massacre at Carlisle in 1537. The promise of a parliament in the north never materialised, and the Reformation would continue under Edward.

Source

(GG) **Despite this apparent failure, the Pilgrimage did come close to success, and an examination of a modern historian's comments about the reasons for its failure may help you to understand what was needed for a successful rising.**

The Pilgrimage of Grace came very close to victory. Indeed, in forcing a truce upon the government in October 1536 and apparently negotiating a settlement in December, the rebels showed signs of being unable to comprehend or exploit their level of success. Crucially, their demands remained limited, their spokesman Robert Aske remained credulous and respectful of the king and the Duke of Norfolk, and the rebels never stirred southwards, enabling Henry to lull his own court into misleading complacency about the extent of the revolt.

Paul Thomas (1999) *Authority and Disorder in Tudor Times 1485–1603.* Cambridge University Press.

ACTIVITY

Read Source GG and answer the following questions.

1   What reasons does Thomas give for the failure of the Pilgrimage?

2   How far do you agree with his interpretation? Why?

Although one of the rebels' targets, Thomas Cromwell, survived in 1536, he fell from power in 1540. It might be argued that the Pilgrimage was the start of Henry's loss of confidence in his chief minister, as he started to realise how unpopular Cromwell's policies were. The rebels may also have succeeded in stopping any further religious changes under Henry, and

even encouraged the conservative reaction that characterised the period from 1539 with the Act of Six Articles and the Act for the True Advancement of Religion (see Chapter 3). This claim to success needs to be balanced against Henry's own religious inclinations. Despite doubts in these areas, it can be argued that the rebels did have some success. First, the scale of the rising was a substantial achievement in itself. The Pilgrimage was the largest rising of the period, drawing in over 40,000 rebels. The rebels were also able to stop the collection of the subsidy and had entry fines set at the level they suggested. Gentry and noble protestors in 1536 called for the repeal of the Statute of Uses; this was achieved in 1540 when it was replaced by the Statute of Wills, which changed the rules of inheritance. Those who rose for economic reasons might therefore have been pleased with the outcome, while those who wanted to reopen the monasteries would have been disappointed. It is also interesting to speculate what would have happened if the Cumberland or Bigod rising of 1537 (see pages 126–130) had not given Henry the opportunity and excuse to exact revenge. Would he have summoned the parliament in the north and met the rebels' grievances?

The Western Rebellion, like the Pilgrimage, did not succeed in reversing the religious changes of the government. The government's brutal response, with the killing of over 3000 rebels, left little doubt that they would accept no opposition to their religious policies, made very clear in the symbolic hanging of Robert Welsh from the church of St Thomas. It would appear that the same failure is true of Kett's Rebellion. At Dussindale, where the rebel army was defeated, over 3000 rebels were killed. Kett was arrested, tried for treason and hanged. The aftermath of the rising saw only 49 known executions, but the government had been more bloodthirsty than the rebels. However, Source HH, a letter from the Privy Council in July 1549, in the name of Edward VI, suggests that the rebels did have some success.

Source

HH **The Privy Council, in the name of Edward VI, writes to the rebels in Norfolk, 18 July 1549. In this letter they try to persuade the rebels that their grievances will be listened to:**

We have been informed that you have assembled in large companies in a very disordered fashion. You have forgotten the Bible which teaches obedience to the King. We have always been ready to address your grievances, and have sent commissioners to reform enclosures. You make humble petition to us for further reform and we will ensure that rents are returned to their old levels. Other reforms will be discussed in the next Parliament. We urge you now to return quietly to your homes.

ACTIVITY

1 What was the purpose of the Privy Council's letter to the rebels?

2 How might this affect its reliability?

3 Using your own knowledge, say how accurate the Privy Council's comments are in their response to the rising.

If the risings are seen as having a social and economic basis, then the results for the rebels are more encouraging. The government passed a variety of measures that did much to improve conditions for the peasantry. The removal of Somerset in October 1549, although not one of the rebels' aims, brought John Dudley, Duke of Northumberland, to the fore. A more able administrator and financier than Somerset, he was able to tackle some of the issues that had precipitated the unrest. He was fortunate that the heat of rebellion had died down and he was able to embark on a policy of redress. His first move was to revalue the coinage in 1551, putting an end to Somerset's policy of devaluation and giving people more confidence in the metallic content of the coinage, bringing greater stability to the economy. He also addressed the problem of sheep-farming and its impact on food prices, particularly in times of distress, by three pieces of legislation. The first, the 1552 Act concerning the re-conversion of tillage to pasture, was followed in 1552 by the licensing of corn dealers and then the systematic collection and disbursal of alms. The programme was completed between 1552 and 1555 by the regulation of the cloth industry, which would help to protect those employed in it.

It is also important to remember that there were many other counties in southern and eastern England where riots and risings had been contained. This raises the question: why did these riots not develop into full-scale unrest, as in Norfolk and the West Country? The answer in some cases is simple: the rebels did achieve their aims. In Suffolk, Sir Anthony Wingfield was able to quell the unrest with pardons and promises of improvements. The same was true in Sussex: at Arundel the rebel leaders were entertained and shown hospitality by Arundel and then they dispersed. In this instance, by being shown the hospitality expected of a member of the ruling class in hard times, the rebels were satisfied and dispersed. The same may be true of many of the enclosure riots that characterised 1549. The rebels tore down the hedges of enclosing landlords; what we do not know is whether the hedges reappeared. If they did not, the rebels had achieved their goal. This form of protest was just one among many open to those who were disgruntled. Before this there would probably have been grumbling about prices, the number of sheep being grazed on common land or the lack of hospitality shown by gentry at a time of shortage. This might have been followed by petitions and legal complaints and then direct action. Only if all else failed might the peasants have resorted to rebellion. The fact that many of the disturbances never got that far suggests that grievances were being resolved at an earlier stage and that the lower orders were having some success in preserving their traditional rights.

It might be argued that Mary Tudor led the only successful rebellion of the period, as she was able to overthrow Queen Jane and re-establish the Tudor dynasty on the throne. This was a remarkable achievement as it appeared that the government held all the cards and should have been able to defeat Mary. Tudor rule was not popular, whereas Northumberland had brought the country peace and stability after the unrest of 1549. Many may also have been willing to ignore the legitimate succession to avoid having another weak and female ruler; others may have wanted to avoid the return to Catholicism that would inevitably follow Mary's accession to the throne. The government held London and in particular the Tower, but had failed to capture Mary: she had escaped from the city before Edward's death and gone to her estates in East Anglia. Mary was successful because she had a legitimate claim, and this was important to all the landed classes, Catholic or Protestant. If they supported an illegal claimant, all laws could be brought into question, and that could threaten their land tenure. It was therefore in their interests to support the rightful ruler, as not doing so would encourage anarchy and a return to 1549. Mary was able to rally both Protestant and Catholic gentry behind her cause. At the same time, her actions reinforced the belief that she was the rightful queen. She proclaimed herself queen and sent letters to the Privy Council and towns throughout the land, informing them of her succession. It was clear that if Northumberland wanted to survive, he would have to fight Mary. Mary's departure from London and rallying of troops meant that Northumberland

had to pursue her, and once he left London his situation deteriorated. Privy councillors who had supported his scheme now had the opportunity to reveal their true feelings and soon fell in behind Mary. Meanwhile, Northumberland was unable to gain the much-needed military support as he moved east, despite increasing his men's pay. In the end he was forced to withdraw and proclaim Mary queen.

Some might argue that these events do not constitute a rebellion and that it was simply the legitimate ruler gaining the throne, yet Jane had been crowned and it did appear, at least for a short time, that England could be thrown into civil war. Even if we reject the idea that Mary staged a successful rebellion, it is possible to argue that Northumberland, in having Jane crowned, staged a successful, albeit short-lived, rebellion in altering the legitimate succession.

It would be difficult to argue that Wyatt's Rebellion in 1554 achieved any success. The aims of the rebellion were religious and political, but neither was successful. Mary restored Catholicism and married Philip of Spain. It could be argued that the rising was always doomed to failure, as it was only 12 months after the Lady Jane Grey affair, when the country had rallied to the legitimate ruler; they were not going to abandon her now. At this time, Mary had not yet adopted the religious policies that would alienate much of the nation, and it is not surprising that so few rallied to Wyatt, even if they had some sympathy for his cause. Despite its defeat, the rebellion did have an impact on the regime, and may well have discouraged the coronation of Philip. This was a serious affront to his dignity and discouraged him from spending time in England, thereby helping to ensure that there was no Catholic succession! The rising also prevented Mary from disinheriting Elizabeth and therefore, in the long term, succeeded in bringing about a Protestant succession. In Parliament, Mary also had to accept that former monastic lands would not be returned to the Church, once again weakening the restoration of Catholicism. In its success in influencing policy through Parliament, the gentry had discovered a better way of bringing about change than rebelling.

The rebellion of the Northern Earls achieved very little. A comparison with the Pilgrimage of Grace shows that the rebels were unable to raise a force of one-eighth the size of that of 1536, suggesting that religious change was no longer such a divisive issue. Elizabeth was able to confiscate so much land from leading northern families such as the Lumleys or Percies, that traditional feudal structures in the north broke down, allowing her to strengthen her hold on the region. The Council of the North was restored and placed under the leadership of the Puritan Earl of Huntingdon. He was given wide powers so that he could take over the government of the north in Elizabeth's name. The failure of the rebellion marked the final settlement of the northern question and gave Elizabeth the opportunity to destroy the autonomy of the region once and for all. As Fletcher argued in *Tudor Rebellions* (2004), 'the failure of the rebellion, its feebleness and its disorganisation, all proved that northern feudalism and particularism could no longer rival Tudor centralisation.'

If the causes of the Northern Rising had any roots in the social and economic problems of the time, it is possible to argue that, as with the risings of 1549, the government's initial reaction of repression was followed by an attempt to tackle some of the issues. The 1572 Vagabonds Act, although enacting severe penalties against vagrants, also showed that the government was aware that the plight of the poor was not always their own fault. Justices of the Peace were to keep a register of the poor in their parish and raise a poor rate to provide shelter for the elderly and sick. Measures such as these and the subsequent 1576 Act did much to prevent widespread unrest in the north during the crisis years of the 1590s, when hunger and starvation were prevalent.

ACTIVITY

Instead of considering the rebellions individually, it is important to see if any themes emerge in terms of their impact on royal authority. This will also help to prepare you for the thematic paper you will study at A2, whatever option you choose to study.

Break down the rebellions under the following headings and consider their impact on royal authority.

a   First, identify the rebellions that fall into each category – note that some will appear in more than one category.

b   Using the information in this section, decide what impact each rebellion had on royal authority.

c   Award the type of rebellion a mark from -5 to +5, depending on whether it strengthened or weakened royal authority (the greater the increase in royal authority, the higher the mark).

Type of rebellion	Rebellion	Impact on royal authority	Mark
Dynastic/deposition rebellions			
Rebellions linked to court coups			
Tax rebellions			
Religious rebellions			
Regional rebellions			
Social/economic unrest			

Having completed the table, you are now in a position to develop your own hypotheses as to the success of rebellions in the period 1536–69.

The following suggestions should help to get you thinking:

◼ Tudor rebellions had little impact on royal authority.

◼ Rebellions that attracted cross-class support had a greater impact on royal authority.

◼ Royal authority increased as a result of rebellion.

◼ Rebellions that threatened the Tudor dynasty were more likely to have an impact on royal authority than those that just wanted a change in royal policy or advisors.

This chapter has encouraged you to develop the skills needed for the final question on the Enquiries paper, where you will need to evaluate a range of sources in order to reach a judgement about a particular issue.

◼ You have seen how to group sources according to whether they support or disagree with an interpretation.

◼ You have developed the skills needed to test the provenance of a source.

◼ You have learnt how to apply your own knowledge to a source or group of sources to test the view they put forward.

◼ You have been encouraged to put forward your own judgement about the issue in the light of the provenance of the sources and your own knowledge.

As a result, you should now feel confident that you have the skills needed to do well on this paper.

Conclusion

Although the period from 1536 to 1569 witnessed many difficulties for the Tudor monarchy, and there were times when it was severely challenged – particularly in 1553 when it was overturned for a short time – it would be very difficult to argue that it was a period of continuous crisis. There may have been individual events that caused, or had the potential to cause, a crisis, and this is for you to judge. Whatever conclusion you reach, it might also be worth thinking ahead and remembering that Elizabeth's reign is often seen as a 'Golden Age', suggesting that if the Tudors were challenged they had been able to survive and leave a strong enough legacy for the state to develop and flourish.

There were political challenges during the period. Most importantly, Henry VIII's failure to leave an adult male heir resulted in fears that the country would return to the chaos of the fifteenth century and the Wars of the Roses. However this did not happen, despite frequent poor leadership, particularly under Somerset. The closest it came was in the summer of 1553 with Northumberland's attempt to alter the succession, but the triumph of Mary suggests that the foundations of the Tudor monarchy were strong and that even self-seeking ministers could not undermine this.

Religiously, the country underwent a vast array of changes, yet unlike much of mainland Europe, England experienced no religious wars. There was a great deal of compromise, particularly under Elizabeth, and her lasting settlement is testament to her ability to prevent the country sliding into the religious chaos that characterised both France and the Netherlands at this time. There were occasions when the country did appear to be heading towards religious unrest, most noticeably in 1536, 1549 and 1569. However, although all of these challenges had the potential to cause crises, the period can be seen as remarkably tolerant, particularly when compared to the religious persecution in Europe. Although there were individuals who were willing to die for their beliefs, the numbers were small and for much of the period the rulers did not want to force people into martyrdom; as a result the worst excesses of religious change were avoided.

The Tudor economy was in a weak state and there were certainly social changes associated with these developments, but it is difficult to argue that it was in a state of constant crisis. There were particularly bad years and under Mary a series of very poor harvests and disease caused serious concern, but these were not so great as to provoke rebellion. Perhaps, just as importantly, the period also witnessed the gradual involvement of the state in tackling social and economic issues. It might be argued that the widespread unrest of 1549 pushed the state into taking greater social and economic responsibility; if this is the case then it can be argued that it helped to prevent serious disquiet and prevent the potential crisis becoming a reality.

It cannot be denied that the period witnessed a significant number of rebellions and many other disturbances. Once again, many of these had the potential to cause a crisis: the Pilgrimage of 1536 produced a force far greater than Henry's, Wyatt got close to entering the City of London and the unrest of 1549 was on a large scale. However, on all occasions the government was able to survive and, if the size of the 1569 rising of the Northern Earls is an indicator, increase its control. This argument appears even stronger if one considers how far the scale of rebellion declined through the rest of the Elizabethan period. Rebels, or potential rebels, either saw the futility of rising or found other means, such as voicing grievances in Parliament, to raise their concerns.

The Tudor state certainly faced difficulties, but to what extent they amounted to crises is open to debate. Perhaps when a number of the potential causes of crisis coincided, the threat was great. If this is true, 1549 might appear to be the most dangerous year for the Tudor state, with political instability, religious reform and social and economic upheaval all leading to widespread unrest and rebellion in much of the country.

Through studying this book and thinking about the events, you should be in a position to reach your own supported conclusions, but as you read more widely and develop your historical skills you should, like any good historian, be willing to modify your views.

ExamCafé
Relax, refresh, result!

Relax and prepare

Charlie

When I started work for this paper I was not really aware that the emphasis was on source skills, so I thought that if I learnt all the facts about the mid-Tudor period I would be able to produce a good answer. It was a real shock when I got my first pieces of work back: I saw that I was not getting marks for simply putting in facts and my teacher said I should not approach this paper as if it was an essay paper in which I used the sources to help me answer the question. My advice to anyone would be focus on the source skills you need, rather than the content.

Hot tips

Lucy

When it came to revision my file of notes was very thin and this worried me. I did not have notes on every bit of the period, but the teacher said it was not needed. She told me to think in terms of debates and the issues. When I started to look at it that way, I realised that I did not need all the details that I had for the other paper.

Sandra

I had found the source paper at GCSE quite straightforward; the information I needed to answer the question was easily extractable from the source as the message was always very clear. However, I soon discovered that the messages in the sources at AS were not as easy to spot and that you needed to read the source very carefully and think what the message was. The sources did not always talk about what was in the question and I needed to avoid simply describing what was in the source.

Freddie

The first part of the course was really hard. I thought that I could do the same as I had done at GCSE and simply say that a source was biased because it was written by Hitler or by the King. I did not explain why it might be biased. When it came to revision I looked back at my early work and realised how bad it was, but I was also able to see how I could improve it. The fact that I knew how to improve it gave me confidence and made me realise how much progress I had made.

Greg

At GCSE it didn't matter as much if you worked through sources sequentially, but at AS I soon discovered that for question (a) you had to compare sources sequentially. I found this quite difficult, but my teacher told me to start by identifying the overall message of the source and asking whether the others were the same or different. This gave me a good way into the comparison and encouraged me to make point-by-point comparisons. It was the same with question (b): I needed to group the sources according to whether they agreed or disagreed with the hypothesis in the question.

Kate

I found point-by-point comparison quite difficult, but the teacher got two of us to go to the front and ask the class to do a comparison. At first I thought 'what is the point of this?' but when we came to do the next comparison question I remembered the activity and it made me answer in a point-by-point way.

Dorcas

I did not find revision very easy as I much prefer learning loads of facts or spider diagrams of reasons, but this paper was a skills paper and I wondered how on earth do I revise for skills? I was also worried that I would be given a set of sources I had not seen before. The best advice I was given was to think about the key debates, such as 'How unstable was England?' and write down all the evidence for it being unstable and all the evidence for it being stable and then develop my view. This was a real help as I was then able to link the debates I had thought about to the sources that were set.

Minh

I couldn't believe how much emphasis this paper had on source skills; it was only when the teacher went through the mark scheme that I realised I needed to evaluate the sources, rather than just write an essay. He also told us to look carefully at the source attribution and date, as that would help us to judge its reliability and perhaps explain why it was written. This was a real help as it kept me focused on the sources rather than simply writing all I knew about the topic.

Ally

It was a real help to consider the debates about the issues we were studying rather than simply learning all the facts. My teacher encouraged me to develop my own view about each issue and then to be able to justify it. This meant that when it came to the exam I had already thought about the issue that the question was on, so I had a view and it was much easier to develop my answer and reach a conclusion. It was also much less of a shock when I opened the paper and saw that I had already thought about the debate.

Jonathan

When we first started doing comparison questions I just used to compare the sources. I didn't compare them as evidence for what was being asked, and therefore I didn't focus on the question. I started to highlight the last part of the question and this helped me to focus on the actual demands of the question and not simply write a general comparison.

James

At first I didn't really understand that to reach the higher marks I needed to compare not only the content of the sources, but also their provenance. The teacher kept saying that I needed more on provenance, but it was only when I went through an answer with two highlighters, one for content and one for provenance, that I realised how little I was writing about provenance. It was the same when we came to question (b): I did not realise how little evaluation of the sources I was doing until I highlighted my answer!

Sarah

I found grouping sources for question (b) really difficult and also I used too much of my own knowledge which I did not link to the sources. Our teacher gave us a chart which asked us to decide if the sources agreed or disagreed with the statement. There was another column for their reliability and finally one for our own knowledge that either agreed or disagreed with the statement. This got me to see which agreed and disagreed and to deal with them together, but also only to bring in knowledge that was directly related to the question. This chart kept me much more focused.

Adnan

I hate revision and I was worried that I would not be able to learn all the key dates for the paper. I used post-it notes all round my room with key dates and events written on them; I found this a real help. I also had a pile of small revision cards, with a date on one side and a key event on the other; this really helped as I could keep testing myself until it all sank in.

Getting started

The exam

In the exam you will be faced with two questions.

The (a) question will always ask you to compare two sources as evidence for something. It is worth 30 marks and you should spend roughly 30 minutes on this question.

That leaves you 60 minutes to deal with the (b) question, which requires you to use all the sources and your own knowledge, and is worth 70 marks.

(a) questions

- You should spend 30 minutes on this answer. Make sure you spend 5–10 minutes planning. Once you know the significant areas of agreement and disagreement, it will not take long to write the answer.

- You do not need to complicate things. Keep your answer clear and focused. The key to getting a top mark is writing about **why** the sources differ/agree, not how they differ/agree, so do not stick with just a basic comparison.

- Begin with a point-by-point comparison, dealing with the sources together, not separately, to make a proper comparison.

- Use short quotations to reinforce your points, but use your own words to explain the points of comparison.

- Always look to compare the sources as evidence for something, which is what the question will require of you.

- Remember that you do not need to use any of your own knowledge explicitly in this question, but you will need to know the context of both sources in order to evaluate them effectively (i.e. what was happening in that year, what happened just before, who the author is and who the recipient of the source is). Think about the situation and purpose of the author and the audience, and look at the date of the source. These issues may well explain the tone and the language used in the source.

Structuring your answer to (a) questions

- The first two paragraphs are comprehension-style accounts of the similarities and differences between the two sources, but make sure you stick to the focus of the question (comparing them as evidence for something).

- The third paragraph, which is the key paragraph, examines the provenance of the sources and why they agree/disagree (situation, purpose and tone).

- Finally, you need to make a judgement in your conclusion as to which of the sources provides the better evidence for what you have been asked. This might be because one source is limited in some way in terms of its provenance or content.

(b) questions

You have left yourself 1 hour to complete the (b) question, which is worth 70 marks. Make sure you leave 10 minutes to plan your answer and to think about which sources agree/disagree with the statement and why that might be the case. The object of the (b) question is to assess how far the sources, with your own knowledge, support an interpretation.

- Highlight the focus of the question and shape your argument around it. Remember that you have to consistently assess how far the sources support the interpretation.

- Group the sources around the focus of the question, so that your approach is analytical, rather than source by source (for example, 'Sources B and D support the interpretation but A and C support it to a lesser extent if at all').

- Remember to evaluate the provenance and reliability of source material as you go along.

- Keep the sense of argument or debate throughout your answer rather than surveying the sources.

- Use short quotations from the sources to illustrate your points, but always explain the point in your own words.

- Integrate your own knowledge as you go along, rather than 'bolting on' a paragraph at the end. Bring in issues or events that are not included in the sources, as long as they are relevant to your argument which refers to the interpretation you are assessing. Do not write a paragraph which is purely knowledge-based and goes off at a tangent to the question, but do use the sources as a means of using your knowledge to explain the events and issues. Keep it short, sharp and relevant.

- Form a balanced judgement on the question in light of the sources.

Writing a plan

- Draw up a table of two columns, one column for sources that agree with the question and one for sources that disagree.

- Fit each source to a column. Some sources might fit both columns because they are ambiguous or implicitly support the interpretation. You must, however, include every source in the table.

- Highlight some key quotations from each source to show how it fits your argument. Use different colours to highlight 'agrees' and 'disagrees', so that you can see them at a glance while you are writing.

- Add points of evaluation to your plan. Look carefully at each author and date. Think about the provenance of each source (you will have done this already for two of the sources in the (a) question). Ask yourself **why** the author was writing, **who** they were writing for and whether they were in a **position** to know about the issue. Look at the language, the tone and the perspective of the author and how they relate to the content.

- Add some relevant knowledge to your plan. This will be information that builds on what is in the sources, expanding on an event or person – maybe the author or recipient – and it will be information that cannot be found in the sources. It may support the sources or may oppose what the sources say in relation to the interpretation you are assessing as a whole. Integrate your information to your argument, rather than putting it at the end.

Structuring your answer

- Make a judgement in the first sentence on 'how far' the sources and your knowledge support the interpretation (e.g. if four out of the five sources support the view, then they support it to a great extent). Set out arguments both in favour of and against the interpretation in the introduction, grouping the sources into those which support/those which oppose the interpretation.

- Then write about those sources which support the interpretation, evaluating their provenance and purpose – bringing in your own knowledge relating to that source and the wider context – supporting the interpretation; finish by prioritising those sources which are the strongest and most informative.

- Next, write about those sources which oppose the interpretation, again evaluating provenance and purpose – bringing in your own knowledge relating to that source and the wider context – supporting the interpretation; finish by prioritising those sources which are the strongest and most informative.

- Conclusion: return to the question and reinforce the original point about how far the sources support/oppose the interpretation (your judgement), using extra knowledge of your own outside the sources and anything you omitted earlier on.

Sample question

Study the five sources on Royal Advisers 1540–1569, and then answer **both** sub-questions.

It is recommended that you spend two-thirds of your time in answering part (b).

(a) Study Sources **A** and **E**.

Compare these sources as evidence for relations between monarchs and their advisers. (30)

(b) Study **all** the sources.

Use your own knowledge to assess how far the sources support the interpretation that advisers could be trusted to serve royal interests between 1540 and 1569. (70)

Source

A **Eight months after the execution of Thomas Cromwell, the French ambassador reports on Henry VIII's opinions of his ministers.**

In his illness, King Henry has a gloomy attitude and an evil opinion of his ministers. He said that most of his Privy Council, while pretending to serve him, were only seeking their own profit. But he knew the good servants from the flatterers, and if God lent him health, he would take care that their plans should not succeed. The King sometimes even blames his ministers for Cromwell's death. He says that, by lies and for little reason, they made him put to death the most faithful servant he ever had.

Charles de Marillac, letter to the Constable of France, 3 March 1541

Source

B **The Privy Council's allegations against the Duke of Somerset, after the successful suppression of the 1549 rebellions.**

Somerset encouraged the common people to revolt. He said: 'Good people, in the name of God and King Edward, let us rise with all our power. We must defend the King and the Lord Protector against gentlemen who would depose the Lord Protector and so endanger the King's royal person. They threaten this because the poor common people, after ill-treatment by the greedy gentlemen, were pardoned this year by the mercy of the King and the goodness of the Lord Protector. Let us fight for him, for he loves the poor people of England.'

Privy Council charges against the Duke of Somerset, 6 October 1549

Source

C The Imperial Ambassador, who was very influential with Queen Mary, reports to the Emperor on the factional rivalries in Mary I's Privy Council.

23 November 1554: *it has proved impossible to reduce the excessive number of councillors, for it created too much bad feeling between the old and recent members of the Privy Council.*

10 February 1555: *the split in the Council has grown. The two factions no longer consult together; some councillors transact no business. Paget is now out of favour with the Queen and most of the Council, so he is often in King Philip's apartments.*

27 March 1555: *the Council is very much divided. Neither Arundel nor Paget attended because of their hatred for the Chancellor, Bishop Stephen Gardiner, and other councillors. When the Chancellor reaches a decision, the others immediately try to defeat it.*

Simon Renard, extracts from letters to Charles V

Source

D Elizabeth I's reported words to William Cecil, when she appointed him as a Privy Councillor on the third day of her reign.

I give you this charge. You shall be a member of my Privy Council and content yourself with working hard for me and my realm. This judgement I have of you, that you will not be corrupted with any manner of gift, and that you will be faithful to the State. I judge that you will give the advice you think best, and not change your view to please my private wishes. I judge that, if you know anything that should be declared to me privately, you will tell only me. You can be certain that I shall keep your secret.

Instructions, 20 November 1558

Source

E Elizabeth's relations with her advisers are commented on by an experienced secretary in the reign of her successor; he was a young child in the 1560s.

Queen Elizabeth ruled using faction and parties, which she created, upheld and weakened according to her own great judgement. In a court dispute in the 1560s, a courtier asked Robert Dudley if he thought he was King. The Queen told Dudley: 'God's death, my lord, I have many servants whom I favour, and if you think to rule here I will restrain you. I will have here but one mistress and no master.' This so alarmed Lord Dudley, that he behaved more humbly long afterwards. She was the absolute and sovereign mistress of her councillors.

Sir Robert Naunton, *Fragmenta Regalia*, published in 1641

Alex's answer to question (a)

Sources A and E provide evidence for the relationships of Henry and Elizabeth and their advisers. Both sources display the self-seeking nature of those involved at Court, such as Privy Councillors. In Source A it is suggested that Henry stated he believed the Privy Council were 'pretending to serve him while seeking their own profit', while Source E claims that Dudley was asked 'if he thought he was king.' These are both examples of how faction dominated much of Tudor politics. During Henry's reign there was much factional fighting between reformers such as Cromwell and Cranmer and conservatives such as Gardiner and Norfolk. Cromwell's execution is an example of this because he was executed for delaying the divorce between Henry and Anne of Cleves. Henry was angry because he wanted to marry Catherine Howard; she was a niece of Norfolk and Cromwell did not want Norfolk to gain favour or to lose it himself. In the same way Dudley and Cecil fought for Elizabeth's favour, with Dudley even being involved in the Northern Rising of 1570 in an attempt to improve his position. **1**

However, both sources also show that the monarch had ultimate control. In Source A Henry states that 'he knew the good servants from the flatterers', showing he is aware of his advisers' self-interest. In Source E, Naunton states that Elizabeth 'was the absolute sovereign mistress of her councillors.' Elizabeth used faction to her advantage by creating a Privy Council that contained both reformers and Catholics and listening to both sides. She would listen to them and then think for a long time, showing that she could not be easily influenced and that the final decision was hers. However, at the start of her reign she did not have full control. In 1560 it was thought she was going to marry Dudley, but the plan had to be abandoned when there was rumour, possibly from Cecil, that Dudley had murdered his wife. Henry also employed both reformers and conservatives to advise him and at the end of his reign there is an example of his control. The conservatives accused Cranmer of heresy, but Henry ordered Cranmer to investigate the charges, suggesting that he had trust in him. **2**

Source A does suggest that Henry lacked control and this is missing from Source E. Source A says that Henry 'blames his ministers for Cromwell's death', suggesting that he lacked control. He feels that his councillors tricked him into executing Cromwell 'by lies and a little reason.' But Elizabeth in Source E states how she has 'many servants whom she favours' and reprimands Dudley, forcing him to be 'humble long afterwards.' However, it could be argued that Henry was in control when he executed Cromwell, but now feels guilty and wants to blame his ministers. The difference could also be explained by the fact that Source A describes the end of Henry's reign in the 1540s when he was perhaps losing control, while Source E describes the start of Elizabeth's reign in the 1560s when she was in control.

1 Examiner comment

The start is reasonably focused, but the sources are used to illustrate or referencing for information. A considerable amount of own knowledge is displayed, but it is not linked to the sources or well focused on the actual question; as a result much of it is stand-alone. The reference to Henry's marriage to Anne of Cleves is left unclear.

2 Examiner comment

Once again the sources are used for illustration and, as in the previous paragraph, although there is some attempt at comparison it is within a referenced framework, rather than evaluative. There is some attempt to balance the extent of royal control, but this is not quite the focus of the question. As before, the student has added a large section of their own knowledge at the end of the paragraph, but it is stand-alone and not linked to the sources.

Example answers

3 Examiner comment

This paragraph illustrates a major weakness of the answer as the candidate does attempt to compare the content of the two sources, but makes no real attempt to compare the provenance. There is a brief mention of the date of Source A, but no more, and this ensures that the answer cannot move above Level III for AO2a.

1 Examiner comment

A well focused start, the answer immediately offers an overview of the interpretations put forward in the two sources. The comparison is made point by point and clearly explains the message being put forward in Source E.

2 Examiner comment

This paragraph continues the focus on similarity and once again the comments are developed and explained. The answer uses only brief extracts from the sources, showing that the candidate is able to select relevant material to support their argument.

3 In conclusion, both sources seem to be similar in their suggestion that Henry and Elizabeth were in control of their advisers and the factional struggles. The monarchs were aware of the interests of the advisers in both sources.

Examiner summary

Although the answer reaches a conclusion that the two sources are similar, it does not reach a judgement as to which source is the most useful as evidence for the issue. The answer contains far too much of the student's own knowledge and not enough focus on the sources.

This answer was awarded 18/30

AO1a Level IV   3

AO1b Level III   5

AO2a Level III   10

Sam's answer to question (a)

In some respects the two sources have a great deal in common. Both imply that the advisers around Henry VIII and Elizabeth were often motivated by their own ambition and interests. Source A states how Henry commented that his Privy Council 'were only seeking their own profit.' Source E states that there were 'factions and parties' at Court, implying that courtiers were in groups designed to further their own desires. **1**

Another similarity is that both sources imply that the monarchs were aware of this situation. Source A remarks that Henry 'knew the good servants from the flatterers', while Source E shows how Elizabeth had 'many servants whom I favour', indicating that both monarchs knew who they could trust at court. **2**

However, the sources differ over the extent of this knowledge. According to Source A, Henry only knew of the flatterers whereas Elizabeth had the power to promote them. According to Source E she 'ruled using faction and parties which she created, upheld and weakened according to her own great judgement.' Therefore the source shows that Elizabeth controlled her courtiers more effectively than Henry. She shouted at Dudley, 'I will have here but one mistress and no master', which made Dudley behave 'humbly long afterwards.' In contrast, Henry believed he was manipulated by his courtiers. He complained that his ministers 'by lies' persuaded him to have Cromwell executed, a course of action that he now regretted as he felt Cromwell had been 'the most faithful servant he ever had'. **3**

Source A puts forward Henry's failing health as the reason why he had less control over his advisers than Elizabeth. Source A comments on 'his illness' and later states that Henry himself bemoaned his weakness, stating that 'if God lent him health' he would control his ministers better. This contrasts sharply with Source E, who comments that Elizabeth was 'the absolute and sovereign mistress of her councillors.' Elizabeth, according to Source E, clearly had no health issues limiting her ability to control her ministers. **4**

Despite Source E's praise of Elizabeth, there are limits to its use as evidence for events at Court. Naunton was not present at Court in the 1560s but was writing over 70 years later, making it unlikely that the account is totally accurate. Indeed few historians would suggest that Elizabeth created factions at Court. Instead Source E appears to be simply a reflection of Elizabeth's glory, as she was remembered as a great ruler long after her death and Naunton is simply reflecting this view. In contrast, the writer of Source A, Marillac, as French ambassador, would have been present at Henry's court and would have known that Henry was suffering from poor health. He would also have been aware of Henry's regrets over Cromwell's execution, while outsiders to the Court would be unaware of both these things. Marillac overlooks Henry's frustrations with Cromwell over the marriage with Anne of Cleves that contributed to Cromwell's fall and only reflects on Henry's view of events. Nevertheless, Source A, with its detailed knowledge of events at court, does appear to be a better piece of evidence of relations between the monarchs and their ministers.

Examiner summary

In the final paragraph the candidate does consider the provenance of both sources. Although this is not integrated into the main body of the answer, it does not detract from its overall quality. The sources are assessed for their strengths and weaknesses before a judgement is reached. The answer does not simply see one source as more useful, but considers the weaknesses of Source E before reaching a balanced conclusion as to which source is more useful as evidence for the relations between monarch and ministers, in other words the final sentence links the material directly back to the question. As a result this answer was awarded full marks.

3 Examiner comment

This paragraph clearly shows that there are also differences between the two passages, the comments are fully developed and explained. Once again the arguments are supported by brief, but relevant extracts from the sources.

4 Examiner comment

In this paragraph the candidate explains why there are differences between the two sources. As with previous paragraphs, the argument is supported by brief comments drawn from the passages, showing the candidate's ability to select focused material.

Alex's answer to question (b)

Sources B, D and E all seem to contain evidence that the advisers of monarchs between 1540 and 1569 could indeed be trusted to serve the royal interest. All the sources show the monarch having personal faith in their advisers to carry out their will. Source B shows this because Somerset encourages the common people to 'rise with all their power in the name of ... King Edward.' Equal dependence is placed upon Cecil by Elizabeth in Source D when she says that she judges that he will content himself 'working hard for me and my realm.' Source E supports the amount of favour that she bestows on such people because the Queen proclaims she has 'many servants whom I favour.' However, we must not take the sources at face value because we see that Somerset's call to protect the King referred to in Source B is in 1549 when allegations were made against him, suggesting that such a call was not the King's will. When we know that one of the 1549 rebellions (the Western Rising) was made directly against some of Edward's reforms, it seems even more improbable that Somerset acted on the King's behalf. However, we must look at how Source B is made up of charges brought against Somerset by the Privy Council. This could suggest that some exaggeration may have taken place in the charges made because the Privy Council had been worried by the 'Good Duke's' obsession with helping the poor. They certainly pick up on this in the charges, claiming that Somerset spoke against the 'greedy gentlemen', then saying that the king 'loves the poor, which was typical of Somerset's view. **1**

Sources A and C disagree with the statement and do not agree that advisers were trustworthy between 1540 and 1569. This is also mentioned in places in Source E. Source B suggests that Somerset encouraged the common people to revolt in his own interests, not those of the King, Source A describes how Henry's advisers were only seeking their own profits in serving the King. However, we should remember that the King's poor health and his concern about the succession may have soured his opinion of his courtiers, making him distrustful. Despite this, the reason for Cromwell's death would suggest that some aspects of Henry's feeling are true: he was executed because he had arranged Henry's marriage to Anne of Cleves. Cromwell wanted to strengthen ties between England and Germany, but did consider the issues Henry would have with Anne's looks. This would suggest a vested interest in the marriage. Source C, supported by Source E, shows a growing rift in the Privy Council because of the rise of reform and conservative councillors. The rift opens from 1554 as bad feeling until March 1555 when the Council is very much divided. The authors of both Sources A and C are likely to be unbiased as both are ambassadors and therefore supposedly neutral. **2**

Overall the sources seem to show that between 1554 and 1569 advisers could not be trusted with royal interests because they let their own interests get in the way. In terms of what we already know, this makes sense because especially during Elizabeth's

---

1 Examiner comment

It is encouraging that the answer groups the sources in a sensible manner. Relevant material from the sources is used to support the argument being put forward, but the ideas would benefit from much greater development. However, the answer is able to integrate the student's own knowledge with source analysis to evaluate the interpretation. The answer also brings in the issue of the provenance of the sources and is able to link this to the answer as well.

2 Examiner comment

The grouping of the sources continues with A and C being seen as disagreeing with the statement, allowing the answer to develop a two-sided argument with analysis. The answer also notes that Sources B and E could also be used to support this side of the argument. There is also some cross-referencing between the sources, some evaluation is attempted using pertinent own knowledge and there is a limited consideration of how authorship might impact on reliability. Once again there is focus on the question. However, the answer does not make use of Source C and the student's use of their own knowledge is limited.

reign there were those such as Dudley who saw the absence of a king as the chance to make themselves important and rule the country.

Examiner summary

The answer reaches a clear, if somewhat brief, conclusion about the interpretation. The judgement reached is somewhat incomplete, but the answer has focused on the question and will be rewarded. There is imbalance between the use of the sources and the student's own knowledge, but the answer has developed a two-sided argument, which is rewarded.

This answer was awarded 47/70

AO1a Level III   6

AO1b Level III   7

AO2a Level II   18

AO2b Level II   16

Sam's answer to question (b)

Sources A and C superficially suggest that advisers could not be trusted to serve royal interests between 1540 and 1569 as there was widespread factional rivalry that influenced the monarch. Sources B, E and D, however, convincingly support the assertion that the advisers worked together and supported royal interests. **1**

Sources A and C put forward the interpretation that the advisers were ambitious and did not try to serve royal interests. Source A states that Henry himself did not feel his councillors were supporting him as 'they pretended' to serve him and did so only for their own profit. There is evidence to support this interpretation as the conservative factions under Norfolk and Gardiner persuaded Henry to execute his chief minister, Thomas Cromwell, who had served him well previously. This infers that they were self-seeking, as by removing Cromwell they were able to have greater influence with the King. The fact that Henry regretted executing Cromwell also suggests that he recognised that it had not been in his own best interests. There is also evidence that Henry's councillors did not serve royal interests at the end of his reign when the radical faction took control of his will and the dry stamp to ensure that Somerset headed the Regency Council of Henry's son, Edward. **2**

However, Source A is limited in its interpretation of events. It was written in 1541 and therefore does not show the end of the reign where Henry successfully outlined the succession and put in place a balanced Regency Council for his son, Edward. There is also no consideration of the role Henry played in the execution of Cromwell so that he could marry the more conservative Catherine Howard. It can therefore be suggested that it was Henry's lust for her, rather than the role of his advisers, that resulted in Cromwell's downfall. **3**

1 Examiner comment

The answer starts by grouping the sources in a sensible fashion, but also offers a view on the interpretation put forward in the question, noting that Sources A and C superficially suggest that advisers could not be trusted, whereas Sources B, D and E are more convincing in supporting the assertion.

2 Examiner comment

The opening suggests that the sources will be considered as a group, but this approach is not pursued. However, Source A is fully explained and the sources are not simply used for reference. The short quotations from the source serve to support the argument and the candidate integrates their own knowledge to support the argument and suggest that the view put forward by Marillac is credible.

3 Examiner comment

This paragraph sees further evaluation of the source, this time by considering its provenance and its limitations. However, even here the answer integrates the student's own knowledge effectively, both by mentioning the Regency Council and developing an explanation for the fall of Cromwell.

Source C also disagrees with the statement that advisers could be trusted to serve royal interests by acknowledging that Mary's council was full of factional disputes and disagreements. By stating that the Council was 'split' and that no decisions were made as an opposing group would always try to defeat them, Renard is suggesting that Mary could not control her councillors and therefore could not successfully impose her views. There is evidence to support this interpretation as her council was very large, with 43 members, and was divided over issues such as Mary's marriage and the reintroduction of heresy laws. **4**

However, this source is limited as this rivalry did not mean that the advisers did not serve Mary's wishes. In practice, the council worked together effectively in 1554 to devise a marriage treaty with Philip of Spain that was very favourable to England. Philip was to be king in name only and was not permitted to drag England into war or have advisers on the Council. Similarly, Renard, being the Imperial ambassador, would exaggerate the problems of Mary's councillors due to jealousy and his desire to have personal influence with the Queen. **5**

Source B suggests that Somerset did protect royal interests as it states that he encouraged the common people to revolt in order to 'defend the King.' It states that Somerset claimed he was fighting for King Edward, who loved the common people, and therefore he felt he was protecting royal interests by encouraging people to revolt. However, Edward's youth made him very susceptible to ambitious councillors and it is possible that Somerset simply claimed that Edward wished people to revolt in order to protect his own position. It is evident that Somerset was fearful of being 'deposed' and therefore he used the King's name to try to save himself. The fact that the source is by the Privy Council, who are charging Somerset, shows that they thought he was lying and therefore his over-ambition infers that he was not serving royal interests. There is evidence to support this as Somerset ruled as a 'quasi' king from his own house and his greed may also have pushed him into acting in his own interests rather than Edward's. However, the source shows only Somerset's Protectorship and fails to take account of the rule of Lord President Northumberland, who served Edward well and involved him in day-to-day decisions. **6**

Sources D and E support the assertion that advisers could be trusted to serve royal interests during Elizabeth's reign. In Source D, Elizabeth shows that she trusts Cecil as she says she regards him highly and trusts his opinion even if it challenges her view. There is a wealth of evidence to support this interpretation, as Cecil became a reliable servant to both Elizabeth and the state. Although Elizabeth was a woman and could have been manipulated by factional rivalry, Cecil prevented this by assuming the position of her Chief Adviser. He did not become over-ambitious and showed that he served royal interests as he was central to the drafting of the Elizabethan religious settlement at

4 Examiner comment

As with the comments on Source A, so the answer fully examines and explains Source C and relates it closely to the question. The evidence quoted from the source is brief but effective. The same is true with the student's deployment of their own knowledge: it is integrated and not simply bolted on in an extensive paragraph at the end of the answer, but is used effectively to answer the question.

5 Examiner comment

In this paragraph the provenance of the source is considered; this time the answer looks at the authorship to assess its reliability. However, the student also uses their own knowledge effectively to assess the reliability.

the start of her reign and enforcing Protestantism. However, it can be argued that he supported 'state' rather than 'royal' interests as he did seize Spanish bullion in the 1560s against Elizabeth's wishes. Nevertheless, Source D shows how strongly Elizabeth trusted her adviser on a personal level, as she asked him to declare his opinion to her and that she would keep his secret and respect him. **7**

Source E also supports the view that advisers could be trusted to serve royal interests, as it states that Elizabeth was in complete control and was the 'absolute mistress' of her councillors. This source argues that Elizabeth used factional rivalry so that every councillor owed allegiance to her and would therefore uphold her interests. It also suggests that her councillors were not overambitious, as Elizabeth asserted her power frequently by saying that she had 'no master', and that they behaved 'humbly' towards her. Elizabeth was able to use her gender and femininity to ensure that she had absolute control. Although some of her councillors wanted her to marry and name a successor in return for a parliamentary subsidy, Elizabeth refused, again indicating her power. However, the writer, Sir Robert Naunton, was only a child during Elizabeth's reign and had only an outsider's view of the situation as he did not work on the council, making the source less credible. **8**

The sources as a set support the interpretation that advisers could be trusted to serve royal interests between 1540 and 1569. There were some ambitious councillors, but the monarchs were able to maintain control throughout the period, even defeating attempts by advisers to change the succession, as happened in 1553. It was the monarch who ultimately made decisions over policy, marriage and the succession, and these were adhered to.

Examiner summary

The conclusion successfully brings together the preceding paragraphs to reach a balanced conclusion. The only weakness here is the failure to refer back to the sources; this is a pity as candidates do need to remember that this is a source paper.

This is a highly convincing and solid evaluation of the sources to answer the actual question set. The knowledge used is balanced, accurate and perceptively applied to the question and not simply bolted on. The answer uses the sources' content and provenance very effectively and the interpretation is at the heart of an answer that brings together the content of the sources and evaluation.

This answer was awarded 64/70

AO1a	10
AO1b	11
AO2a	24
AO2b	19

6 Examiner comment

This paragraph, unlike the previous ones, deals with both an analysis of the content of the source and its provenance. The answer continues to explain the sources and does not simply use them to illustrate the answer or for reference. A number of issues concerning the provenance are considered, including authorship and purpose as well as the limitations of the content, and once again the student's own knowledge is integrated into the answer.

7 Examiner comment

The paragraph effectively integrates the student's own knowledge to support the view expressed in the source. There is also a subtlety in differentiating between serving the monarch and serving the state, and this approach is effectively explained.

8 Examiner comment

As in the other paragraphs, the source is thoroughly explained and linked to the question and short quotations are used to support the argument, again showing a clear understanding of the interpretation. There is also evaluation of the provenance in a short, but valid, final sentence.

Bibliography

General (suitable for AS)

Fellows, N. (2005) *Henry VIII*. Collins.

Fellows, N. (2004) *Elizabeth I*. Collins.

Guy, J. (1988) *Tudor England*. OUP.

Loades, D.M. (1992) *The Mid-Tudor Crisis 1545–1563*. Macmillan.

Murphy, D., Keen, A., Tillbrook, M. and Walsh-Atkins, P. (1999) *England 1485–1603*. Collins.

Turvey, R. and Heard, N. (2006) Edward VI and Mary:
A Mid-Tudor Crisis? 1540–1558. Hodder.

Turvey, R. and Heard, N. (2009) *Change and Protest 1536–88: Mid-Tudor Crises?* Hodder.

Turvey, R. and Randell, K. (2008) *Henry VIII to Mary I; 1509–1558*. Hodder.

Williams, P. (1995) *The Later Tudors 1547–1603*. OUP.

How well served was the monarchy?

Bush, M.L. (1975) *The Government Policy of Protector Somerset*. Edward Arnold.

Hoak, D. (1980) 'Rehabilitating the Duke of Northumberland', in J. Loach and R. Tittler (eds) *Mid-Tudor Polity c.1540–1560*. Macmillan.

MacCulloch, D. (1996) *Thomas Cranmer*. Yale.

Randell, K. (1991) *Henry VIII and the Government of England*. Access.

Smith, A.G.R. (1991) *William Cecil, Lord Burghley: Minister of Elizabeth*. Headstart History.

How significant were the religious changes?

Duffy, E. (1992) *The Stripping of the Altars*. OUP.

Duffy, E. (2001) *The Voices of Morebath*. Yale.

Haigh, C. (1993) *English Reformations: Religion, Politics and Society under the Tudors*. OUP.

MacCulloch, D. (1999) *Tudor Church Militant: Edward VI and the Protestant Reformation*. Penguin.

Whiting, R. (1998) *Local Responses to the English Reformation*. Macmillan.

What were the effects of social and economic change?

Coleman, D.C. (1977) *The Economy of England 1450–1750*. OUP.

Heard, N. (1992) *Tudor Economy and Society*. Hodder.

Pound, J.F. (1971) *Poverty and Vagrancy in Tudor England*. Longman.

Slack, P. (1988) *Poverty and Policy in Tudor and Stuart* England. Longman.

What was the nature of the challenge to royal authority?

Beer, B.L. (1982) *Rebellion and Riot: Popular Disorder in England during the reign of Edward VI*. Kent, Ohio.

Bush, M.L. (1996) *The Pilgrimage of Grace*. Manchester.

Caraman, P. (1994) *The Western Rising, 1549: Prayer Book Rebellion*. Westcountry Books.

Cornwall, J. (1977) *The Revolt of the Peasantry*. Routledge and Kegan Paul.

Fellows, N. (2001) *Disorder and Rebellion in Tudor England*. Hodder.

Fletcher, A. and MacCulloch, D. (1997) *Tudor Rebellions*. Longman.

Hoyle, R.W. (2001) *The Pilgrimage of Grace*. OUP.

Land, S.K. (1977) *Kett's Rebellion*. Boydell.

Loades, D.M. (1965) *Two Tudor Conspiracies*. Cambridge.

Glossary

Anabaptists – Protestant extremists, most notable for their activities in the north German town of Munster, where they had introduced communism and polygamy. They burned books, apart from the Bible, and were willing to put unbelievers to death.

anti-clerical – Opposed to the influence of power of the Church.

apprenticeship – A period of time spent by a student (apprentice) learning his trade from a master craftsman.

Black Death – The bubonic plague arrived in England in 1349. It was carried by rats on ships, and killed somewhere in the region of 30 per cent of the population.

Benedictine House – A monastic house that followed the rule of St Benedict, an Italian monk of the fifth and sixth centuries. He drew up a set of rules for monastic life, which was to be the basis of the rules of all monastic orders in the Western Church.

Bill of Attainder – A declaration by Parliament that a person was guilty of treason. This would happen without a trial. The declaration also applied to the person's heirs and would mean the loss of the family estate.

Black Death – The bubonic plague arrived in England in 1349. It was carried by rats on ships, and killed somewhere in the region of 30 per cent of the population.

books of hours – Books that contained prayers to be said at certain times of the day.

catechism – A religious book on key aspects of belief, set out in a question-and-answer form.

chantries – Small chapels where prayers for the dead were said to reduce their time in purgatory.

Church ales – Fundraising banquets that provided the Church with most of its income.

Church calendar – The yearly cycle of religious festivals.

churchwarden's accounts – Churchwardens were responsible for the finances of a church. Their accounts can often be used to show how far they followed the government's instructions.

common land – Village land where everyone who was not a landowner could gather wood and berries and graze their animals.

communion cup – A goblet in which members of the congregation would receive the wine at the Eucharist.

copyholders – Landowners who leased their land over a long period and could pass it on to their children.

Council – The ministers and advisors who were now running the country as Edward VI was too young to rule. However, Somerset largely ignored them and ruled on his own.

debasement – A reduction in the silver content of the coinage and its replacement with a cheaper metal. This yielded enough silver to enable the government to mint more money.

devise – In a monarch's will, a clause that deals with the question of who will succeed to the throne.

diocese – The area of administration under the control of a bishop.

Dry Stamp – A stamp of the royal signature. It could be printed on documents and inked over by clerks. At the end of Henry's reign it was used to sign documents without the King's knowledge, allowing Somerset to exercise a great deal of power.

English sweat – A form of influenza.

engrossing – The redistribution of small pieces of land so that the landowner could have all of his land together in one place.

extreme unction – The anointing of a dying person with holy oil, similar to the anointing of a priest at ordination.

First Book of Common Prayer – This was written by Cranmer and was to be used from June 1549. It was in English and adopted a moderate view of the Eucharist service. There is greater reference to the contents on page 75.

forestalling – Buying up goods in order to sell them at a higher price at a later date.

Hanseatic League – An organisation of German merchants from ports on the Baltic; who had come together to protect their trade. They dominated the trade of much of northern Europe.

Holy Days – Annual saints' days, which were holidays from work. There were often religious ceremonies and processions on these days. Protestants wanted to end them as they believed they encouraged laziness.

homilies – Government-produced sermons so that uneducated priests had ready-made sermons available. They were used to put across key beliefs, such as obedience.

Hunne Case, 1541 – Hunne was a London merchant who refused to pay the required fees to the Church on the death of his son. He was later found murdered in a Church prison, and although no member of the clergy was convicted of his murder, it was generally believed that a clergyman had killed him. The case was used by many historians as an example of Church corruption, but more recently historians have seen the incident as an exception.

husbandry – The management and farming of the land.

indigent – The very needy who lacked even the basic necessities.

injunctions – A series of orders and instructions issued by Thomas Cromwell to priests about what should be taught and the decoration in churches. They were used to promote the new religion.

living – A church office which brought its occupier an income.

Lord's Prayer, Creed, Ten Commandments – These set out the basic beliefs and prayers of the church. If these were in English, everyone would be able to understand them.

militia – Local forces made up of commoners. They were not professional soldiers, but were required to train for a number of days per year.

papal legate – An envoy of the Pope. Pole was the Pope's representative in England.

prayers for the dead – It was believed that praying for the souls of the dead could reduce their time in purgatory.

primers – Small books that set out basic religious beliefs, much like a textbook.

purgatory – It was believed that in order to go straight to heaven, a soul had to be free from sin. Most were not, and so went to a halfway place: purgatory. They would stay there until they were ready to go to heaven; the length of time depended upon the sins they had committed.

rack-renting – Making exorbitant increases in the rent on land.

Real Presence – The belief that in the mass the body and blood of Christ were present in the bread and wine.

Regency Council – A group of councillors who rule on behalf of a monarch while the monarch is a child or a minor. The Regency Council of 1547–49 was headed by Somerset.

regrating – Buying up commodities in advance so as to sell them later at a much higher price. By buying up the goods the merchant created a shortage and so forced up the price.

Rogationtide – A religious festival where crops were blessed and prayers were said for the harvest.

Salic Law – A law that had its origins in France and excluded females from succeeding to the throne.

salvation – Avoidance of hell and entry to heaven.

Smithfield – A marketplace in London where many Protestants were burnt at the stake.

sung mass – A service similar to the usual mass, but the main prayers were sung in Latin rather than spoken.

tenants-at-will – Occupants of land who had no rights and could be forced off it at the will of the landowner.

vagrants – The wandering poor, who roamed the country either looking for work or, as the government believed, causing unrest.

Valor Ecclesiasticus – A record of the wealth and income of the Church. Cromwell had sent out commissioners in 1535 to collect these details.

visitation – This was like an inspection. The visitors would question the monks about the monastery and then write a report for Thomas Cromwell.

Index